JUST IN TIME

LENTEN SERVICES

Lucy Lind Hogan

Abingdon Press
Nashville

JUST IN TIME!
LENTEN SERVICES

This book is printed on acid-free paper.

Library of Congress Cataloging-in-Publication Data

Hogan, Lucy Lind, 1951-
    Lenten services / Lucy Lind Hogan.
        p. cm. — (Just in time)
    Includes bibliographical references and index.
    ISBN 978-0-687-65516-8 (binding: pbk., adhesive perfect : alk. paper)
    1. Lent. 2. Worship programs. I. Title.

BV85.H633 2008
264—dc22

                                                                        2008015356

09 10 11 12 13 14 15 16 17 18—10 9 8 7 6 5 4 3 2 1
MANUFACTURED IN THE UNITED STATES OF AMERICA

For

my Parents

Wilfred and Margaret Lind

and my Godmothers

Geraldine Rogers and Lucy Gemlo

TABLE OF CONTENTS

CHAPTER ONE

THE JOURNEY TO THE CROSS

A t the center of our lives as Christians are the passion, death, and resurrection of Jesus the Christ. At the center, therefore, of our worship together, spiritually, and very often physically, is the cross; the cross on which Jesus willingly gave his life that we all might have life and have it abundantly. The passion, death, and resurrection are also at the center of the church year. Every Sunday is a little Easter and the cyclical organization of the liturgical year focuses around the retelling of the Passion narrative and the surprising great good news of the Easter acclamation, "Christ is risen; the Lord is risen indeed!" Therefore, each year during Lent, we join Jesus on the journey to the cross, and it is a journey into which we all have been invited. "Pick up your cross," commands Jesus, "and follow me." It is the cross of love and discipleship, faithfulness and devotion, repentance and renewal.

FORTY DAYS OF PURPOSE

Evangelical pastor Rick Warren has had great success lately inviting individuals and congregations into forty days of purpose.

During those forty days people are invited to reflect upon God's story and God's call to them and the meaning of their lives. Lent, however, is the original forty days of purpose. For most of its history, the church has understood Lent to be the time when people were called to do just that, reflect on the purpose of their lives in Christ, where they had gone astray, and how they might rejoin Jesus on the journey toward wholeness and fulfillment in God.

In each community of the faithful we will find people at every stage of the Christian journey. Some are, to use Paul's image, milk Christians (see 1 Cor 3:2). New to the faith, they have yet to hear all of the gospel stories or to shape their lives in this way of the cross. Others, although they may have been a part of the community for a long time, have left the path of Christ for a variety of reasons. Wandering away, they are the lost sheep Jesus was sent to recover. And others, to return to Paul, are solid meat Christians. They are ready to explore and wrestle with the difficult questions. They want to know what it means to pick up their cross. They want to know who is their neighbor and how they might meet the needs of those neighbors. They want to deepen their life in the one who gave his life for them.

As a part of its preparations for the glorious celebration of Easter, the church called for a period of reflection, renewal, penitence, and preparation. The forty days of Lent that begin with Ash Wednesday and culminate in Holy Week, the week of the Passion, are a time not only for those who are already Christians but also for those seeking to become the adopted children of God through baptism, to enter into this journey with Christ.

In this book we will explore the nature and character of the worship and preaching of the services of Lent beginning with Ash Wednesday. How might we shape our prayers and our preaching in ways that will encourage reflection and preparation? How will we help our congregations to set off on the journey so that, as they arrive at Easter, they might fully join their voices with the witnesses in every generation who have joyously proclaimed that "Christ is risen," and that they "have seen the Lord"?

PREPARATION FOR PASCHA

It took several centuries to arrive at a church year that looks something like the liturgical calendar that we follow today. For the first two centuries the focus was only on Easter or *Pascha*, which was tied to the Jewish observance of the Passover. It was during those events that Jesus had been arrested, tried, and crucified, and it was that story that the church told over and over again.

The community knew that it was important to tell and retell the *Pascha* story of Christ's passion and resurrection each and every time they met. That story gave them their identity, their purpose, and their future. And, unlike their Jewish ancestors who celebrated the Passover but once a year, they quickly decided that they must celebrate their "Passover" through death into life each and every week.

Sunday became the "Eighth Day," the "Day of the Lord," the day on which they told the story of the resurrection and shared the meal as Jesus had commanded them. It was the little Easter. Yet the yearly celebration of Easter was the center of the Christian year and all other seasons of the church year expanded from that day—to the fifty days of Easter, Pentecost, Christmas, and Advent.

The Lenten period served several purposes. One was preparation for the celebration of the Easter Vigil. It was a period of fasting—abstaining from eating meat, and, if possible, a pilgrimage to Jerusalem and the opportunity to pray at the actual sites. But there does not seem to have been any consistency as to how long the fast was to last or what was involved in the preparations.

Lent also became the period of intense preparation for those individuals who were going to be baptized and welcomed into the church at the Easter Vigil—the lengthy service that occurred over Saturday night into Sunday morning. After at least three years of catechesis, education, and testing, those deemed worthy and ready for initiation entered into this final period leading up to the vigil that included fasting and exorcisms. How long this period should last was the subject of lengthy debate, with the church finally settling in on a period of forty days that would have to begin on a Wednesday since the Sundays preceding Easter were not to be considered fasting days. A tradition had already developed of fasting forty days in Epiphany, following the observance of the baptism of Jesus. Those forty days were to imitate Jesus' forty days of testing in the wilderness.

Finally, Lent was a period of penitence for those whose actions were considered sinful and had separated them from God and the community. People were enrolled in the Order of Penitents. They were given the opportunity, through fasting and acts of public penance, to make ready for readmission to the community at the Easter Vigil.

Through this lengthy process of historical development, those of us in the Western churches have arrived at the contemporary interpretation of Lent—the forty days of preparation that precede the celebration of Easter. Lent begins on Ash Wednesday, six-and-a-half weeks before Easter. It is counted as forty days because Sundays are excluded from the count. Easter, being a moveable feast—the first Sunday after the first full moon following the vernal equinox—means that Ash Wednesday is also moveable and can occur as early as February fourth and as late as March tenth.

WALKING THE WAY OF THE CROSS IN THE FOURTH CENTURY

In 383 CE, a woman named Egeria joined a group of pilgrims traveling to participate in the Paschal events and liturgies in Jerusalem. Her journal accounts of those observances give us an invaluable record of how early Christians sought to join Jesus on the way of the cross. On Palm Sunday, they gathered before the tomb of Lazarus. The following day they walked the path of the procession of Jesus' triumphal entry into Jerusalem, waving their palms as the people had done centuries before. Throughout the week, Egeria tells us, they walked and prayed, telling the story and recalling Jesus' actions during the "Great Week." Those

4

were, they knew, historical events, the actions of a real man who had picked up and carried a real cross.

So, during that week, that holy week, the pilgrims sought to join their savior on that real journey. They walked the *Via Crucis* or *Via Doloros*. They gathered in the headquarters of Pilate. They walked through the streets of Jerusalem, where Jesus had walked. They stopped where he fell and where he grieved over the women of the city, and they stood on the hill outside the gates. On Good Friday the pilgrims gathered for a vigil before a portion of the true cross. And finally, on Saturday evening, they observed the Great Vigil.

Egeria's story was foundational as the church developed its worship life together. If you would like to read more about her travels you might read her own words in *Egeria: Diary of a Pilgrimage*, translated by George Gingras (New York: Newman Press, 1970). You may also find more information about her in Maribel Dietz's book, *Wandering Monks, Virgins, and Pilgrims* (University Park, Penn.: Penn State University Press, 2005) and James White's book, *A Brief History of Christian Worship* (Nashville: Abingdon, 1993).

WALKING THE WAY OF THE CROSS IN THE TWENTY-FIRST CENTURY

Jesus calls each of us to pick up our cross and follow him. How might we, who are the followers of Christ, enter into Lent today? How can we use these forty days to deepen our lives in and with Christ, with our neighbor? How might we, who have been called to be disciples, use these days of preparation and penance as an opportunity to walk the way of the cross, to join Jesus in the journey to the cross?

The Journey—Instant and Immediate?

An invitation to the lengthy Lenten journey of preparation may be problematic for people today. We live in a world that expects and demands the instant and immediate. We become impatient if we have to wait at all for anything. A visit to a grocery store tells us that we want instant oatmeal, instant coffee, and minute rice. Most of us have come to rely on our microwave to boil our water and pop our corn.

Computers, likewise, while wondrously expanding our world and possibilities, have also made us annoyed with anything that is less than instantaneous. We instant-message and text, and communicate with people all over the world in the blink of an eye. Whether it is buying tickets for a popular movie, making dinner or airline reservations, or registering for a college class, we depend on the computer to do it quickly and efficiently. We bank and pay bills online anytime of the day or night. Instantly and immediately we know our bank balance and take care of all of our business.

While we may not yet have achieved the mode of travel envisioned in the Star Trek series, the distances on our globe have shrunk tremendously. We now think nothing of traveling across the country or across the ocean. What used to take weeks now takes only a matter of hours. For most of us, the concept of a journey is no longer arduous or life threatening. We board a plane in New York, and five hours later we step off in Los Angeles.

As wonderful as this all is, it has the potential to make it difficult to invite people to a less-than-"instant" journey to the cross. We are speaking to an "I want it and I want it *now*" world. But that is not what Lent is about. It is about entering into a gradual, deliberate journey of instruction, self-reflection, examination, and reparation.

Fasting—Watermelon and Candy?

Many people have a rather limited understanding of Lent. They view it only as a time to give up something we like—candy, desserts, or television.

I had a seminary colleague who always gave up watermelon for Lent. He loved watermelon but knew that he was safe in giving up a summer fruit during the spring. In those days watermelons were only available in the summer. Consequently, the chances of being tempted to break his Lenten fast were fairly slim.

Our Lenten journey, although it may include abstaining from certain foods or activities as a way of reminding us of what we are doing, can be much more than that. It can be a time for us to realize the purpose of our life and to deepen our relationship with the one who gave his life for us. The traditional understanding and Lenten practices of the early church provide us with rich possibilities as we seek to journey to the cross.

Preparing for Baptism

While most churches will not want to return to the early church's tradition of only baptizing new members at the services of Easter or Pentecost, Easter can be an excellent time to bring new members into church and bring them into the waters of baptism as the church celebrates the movement of death into life. Lent could then return to one of its earliest purposes, preparing individuals for baptism.

In addition to the Sunday services during Lent, the six-and-a-half weeks can be a time to provide educational opportunities. Newcomers to the faith would be able to explore the scriptures, the church's story, what it means to be a Christian, and what it means to live the Christian life.

Lenten Disciplines: Deeper and Deeper in Our Faith

Lent is a time to bring new people into the church, but it is also an opportunity for those who have already been baptized and have become members of the body of Christ to deepen their relationship with Christ and with the other members of the church. Consequently, the catechetical courses offered to those preparing for baptism would also be a wonderful opportunity for others to learn more about and grow in their faith.

Lent is not only about fasting and denial—giving up eating certain foods or eating meat on Friday—undertaking abstinence can be another way for people to grow and deepen their faith.

The purpose of such an approach is not punishment; it is a reminder of the days of preparation and the end of the journey, the death and resurrection of Christ.

Giving alms has always been an important Lenten discipline. Lent might also be a time for individuals as well as congregations to take on new projects and missions. It is a time to become aware of the neighbor and strangers who are in need. How is God calling us to meet the needs of those other children of God?

The Broken Made Whole

Finally, Lent can be a period of self-reflection and examination. How have we failed to live the life that God would have us live? How do we neglect and ignore our neighbor? It is a time to uncover our brokenness, our finite nature, and the ways that we live incomplete, imperfect lives. We must not deny or avoid the reality of sin in our lives and in the world around us. Only by confronting the principalities and powers that seek to overwhelm us will we come to the end of our journey understanding that "neither death, nor life, nor angels, nor rulers, nor things present, nor things to come . . . will be able to separate us from the love of God in Christ Jesus our Lord" (Rom 8:38).

Cleaning House— The Lenten Environment

Egeria and her companions were able to enter into their Lenten journey surrounded by the streets and buildings of Jerusalem. Most of us, however, are not able to travel to the Holy Land for our Lenten pilgrimage. Therefore, an important goal of those planning and conducting worship is to prepare a proper Lenten environment that will allow people to participate more fully in the journey.

As Jewish families prepare to celebrate the eight days of Passover, they begin by cleaning their homes. They sweep in every corner. They clean out the cupboards. All this cleaning is an effort to remove anything, even a crumb that is leavened. During the days when they will be both recalling and living their hasty departure from Egypt and their Passover from slavery into freedom through God's gracious deliverance, they are to eat only matzoth—unleavened bread.

As your community prepares for Lent then, is a time to clean house—to remove the clutter and dust. If your community worships in a more traditional space, Lent should be a time of stark emptiness. If the normal elements that decorate the worship space are removed, people will have a visual reminder that they are involved in a time of intense reflection, repentance, and contrition. The decoration, or lack thereof, will stand in sharp contrast to the superabundance of flowers and festive hangings and vestments of Easter.

Where flowers normally are placed in the worship space, they should either be removed or replaced with simple, bare branches. The seasonal hangings for Lent should be either purple or a rough cloth such as burlap.

If your community worships in a more contemporary space, similar efforts might be made. Hangings of rough, neutral-colored cloth and arrangements of branches will be visual signals that something is happening. If you place trees in your worship space at Christmas and lilies at Easter, then it is important to modify your worship environment during Lent.

FAT TUESDAY

The remaining chapters of this book are devoted to exploring the services that will help us, as the children of God, pick up our crosses and follow our Lord as he walks toward the hill of Golgotha. This journey will be one of penitence, fasting, and self-examination. But, before we set off on that journey, Christians have one other way of cleaning their houses. We are not looking for crumbs of leavened bread, but for fats, rich foods, and meats. And we remove those prohibited items by eating them.

The week or two before Ash Wednesday is known as *Carnival* or *Mardi Gras*. Carnival is from the Latin meaning to "put away flesh (meat)." Mardi Gras is French—"Fat Tuesday:" the day before Ash Wednesday when people enjoy revelry and partying to "put away" food and drink that they will not eat during the next six weeks. We are familiar with the weeks of parties and parades held in New Orleans. But all the festivities stop abruptly at midnight as Ash Wednesday begins and the streets are emptied of revelers.

As your congregations prepare for Ash Wednesday and Lent, they might think about sponsoring a joyous dinner to "put away" the rich foods that they won't eat during Lent. One doesn't have to travel to New Orleans or Rio de Janeiro to host a Carnival or *Mardi Gras*. Some churches hold a pancake supper on Tuesday— to get rid of the eggs and butter.

The Tuesday before Ash Wednesday is also known at Shrove Tuesday. This comes from the Old English word for being forgiven of one's sins. To *shrive* means to forgive. This was the day on which people went to confession before the start of Lent.

USING THIS BOOK

Unlike many worship books that offer you prepared services that you will use in your community, I believe that every worship service must be prepared for a particular people at a particular time. In this book you will find suggestions for some of the elements of your worship service. But primarily I am offering you the resources to help you reflect on and plan your own worship service.

Where does our worship planning begin? Before choosing the music or settling on the hangings with which you will vest the worship space to provide a Lenten atmosphere, I would encourage all those involved in planning worship—clergy, lay worship leaders, lay leaders, lay readers, music ministers, choir directors, musicians, and artists—to enter into a time of Bible study. By gathering as a group, exploring and wrestling with the texts, you will hear God's word spoken anew.

In preparation for the worship-planning Bible study, read the Lectionary texts that are assigned for each service—Ash Wednesday and all of the Sundays in Lent, then gather to examine and discuss those texts. Reflect not only on the biblical texts but put them in the context in which they will be read. What is happening in your congregation, your community, and your world? Every year, every Ash Wednesday and Lenten journey will be undertaken in a very different context. That context must become a part of your conversation. Therefore, in each chapter, I will begin by first discussing the Bible texts that will shape that worship service and the sermon for the day, and I encourage you to do the same.

I will then offer you several themes that are drawn from the readings for the week. These will serve as possible themes around which you might center your service. I will also suggest music selections that grow out of those themes. Finally, I will suggest some prayers and ways to shape the service. I hope that you will use these to stimulate your own thinking and planning.

SETTING OFF ON THE JOURNEY

In the next chapter we will discuss the start of the Lenten journey—Ash Wednesday. May this be a time for you and your congregation to enter more deeply and more fully into life in Christ.

ASH WEDNESDAY

BEGINNINGS

E very journey has a beginning. There is always that moment when one leaves behind the known and the familiar and starts into the new and the unknown. Even if one knows the end point—the destination—one isn't always sure what one will encounter along the way, what new experiences and new insights will present themselves. As Christians setting off on the journey to the cross, we can be sure that Jesus is the way, the truth, and the life. He has gone and goes before us, leading the way. And he travels with us, supporting and encouraging us every step of the way. So, every year on the Wednesday six-and-a-half weeks before Easter Day, the church, the body of Christ, once again sets off on its Lenten journey. While we know that the cross, and ultimately resurrection, are our destination, we do not know what experiences and insights will meet us on our journey.

Throughout the Gospels Jesus reminds us repeatedly how important it is to prepare and take stock of who you are and of what you are capable. Before you go out to wage battle, before you begin to build a tower, before you begin your watch for the much-anticipated bridegroom, you must decide whether you have enough men or money or oil to finish the task.

MARKED WITH ASHES

"You are dust, and to dust you shall return" (Gen 3:19; see 18:27). Are the members of the community familiar with the Ash Wednesday tradition of marking the forehead with ashes? While this marking is an ancient tradition of the church, it is, for many people, something with which they are unfamiliar. People may have many questions and will be unclear why this is done on Ash Wednesday. Therefore, if you are introducing this ritual in a congregation for the first time, it is important that the congregation is educated ahead of time as to what will happen and why. What is the history behind this action and what are the theological reasons for doing this?

Dust and ashes are signs of our humanity. God created us out of the earth. But throughout the scriptures, ashes also serve as signs of mourning and grief. When Joshua grieved for the people who had been killed, he tore his clothing and put dust on his head (Josh 7:6). Job, mourning the death of his children, sat on the ash heap (Job 2:8). And his friends, coming to comfort him, threw dust in the air and on their heads when they saw the state he was in (Job 2:12).

Ashes were also outward and visible signs of confession. Nehemiah and the people of Israel fasted, dressed in sackcloth, and put earth on their heads as they sought to atone for their sins before God (Neh 9:1). And Job, when confronted by God, declared, "I despise myself, and repent in dust and ashes" (Job 42:6).

You might explore with your congregation the modern ways that we grieve or show remorse. For example, while we may no longer fling dust on our heads as a sign of mourning, we do have ways of demonstrating our pain. People now bring flowers, balloons, or stuffed animals to mark the sight of a fatal accident. What are ways the people in your community observe the death of someone?

PREPARING THE ASHES

The preparation for the Ash Wednesday service may actually begin a year before. Centuries ago the custom developed of marking an ashen cross on the forehead of each person. Growing out of the biblical tradition of anointing one's head with ashes, it is to remind us that we "are dust and to dust we will return" and that we are sinners in need of repentance. The ashes that are used come from burning the dried palm branches left from the previous year's Palm Sunday celebration.

While ashes may be purchased from a religious supply company, as the congregation begins its Ash Wednesday/Lenten preparations, it might devote a special time to the burning of the palms that it has saved from the previous year's Palm Sunday celebration and the preparation of the ashes. The congregation might hold a Carnival dinner shortly before Ash Wednesday. At the close of the evening, as the congregation turns its attention to the start of Lent, it could mark that transition by burning the palms.

A practical note is in order. The burning must take place out of doors—away from anything flammable. The palm branches, while dry, tend to smolder rather than burn. The children will be most interested in this activity, but it must be done by an adult and with a fire extinguisher handy. Unfortunately, even after the palms have burned, you will not be left with neat ashes. The next step is to grind them, preferably with a mortar and pestle and then add a bit of olive oil so that they don't fly about. Don't worry—you will not need many ashes, even for a large congregation. (By the end of this effort you may decide that purchasing them from a supply house may not be such a bad idea the next time around. But it does give the congregation a wonderful experience of making the connection between the Ash Wednesday service and the Passion of Jesus.)

SITTING WITH THE TEXT

There will be different sets of lessons for each of the three Lectionary cycles for the Sundays in Lent, but that is not the case for Ash Wednesday. The same set of lessons is read each year.

Joel 2:1-2, 12-17

There are two possible Old Testament scriptures for Ash Wednesday. The first is from the second chapter of Joel. The prophet recognizes the need to summon the people of God to a time of fasting, weeping, and mourning. They have not been living their lives according to God's plan and, as the Day of the Lord approaches, the people, all people—men, women, even children—need to turn away from their sinful ways and return to God. Calling for the raucous, alarming noise of trumpets, Joel wants to make sure that he has the people's attention. He wants to wake everyone, making sure that they have heard his message, that they have been warned.

This passage from Joel may have served a liturgical purpose and we are correct to be reminded of the opening of the Jewish observance of Rosh Hashanah and high holy days that end at Yom Kippur. They begin with the blowing of the shofar, a ram's horn. Might we learn something from that practice? Should our Ash Wednesday services begin, not in silence, but with a loud call to summon us to the journey? In the Gospel reading from Matthew, we will be warned not to blow the trumpet, but there the trumpet was not to sound an alarm, it was to call attention to the person giving a gift in the temple. If we answer Joel's request, we sound the trumpet or shofar to call people back to God.

In addition to alerting us to the journey ahead, the passage in Joel serves as a reminder of what is involved in that journey. It is to be a time of fasting. It is to be a time when we repent of our sins, turning away from those things that keep us from God and returning to the God who loves us. It is crucial, therefore, to lift up not only the images of weeping, mourning, and tearing of garments but also the image of God presented by Joel.

Joel puts before us not only a call for repentance but also the reminder that we follow a God who will listen and accept our contrition and remorse. We are not to wallow in grief, afraid of a vengeful God. No, ours is a God who is "gracious and merciful, / slow to anger, and abounding in steadfast love" (Joel 2:13). Ours is a God who does not want to punish us. And so, we begin our journey toward one who wants to welcome us with open and loving arms.

Isaiah 58:1-12

An alternative to the text from Joel comes from the proclamation of Deutero-Isaiah. Like Joel, the prophet demands the attention of the people. The rebellion of the people calls not for meditative silence but for loud shouting, "Lift up your voice like a trumpet!" When you see people in danger, you do not whisper your alarm. No, you do anything to get their attention—shout, whistle, and wave your arms. That is how we are to open our message.

The message of the prophet is not only to call for a fast but also to instruct his people in the proper way to fast. God does not want them to enter into a fast that is focused on themselves rather than God. It is not enough merely to make an outward change—bowing one's head and wearing sackcloth and ashes. Rather, God wants an inward change.

The reading from Isaiah is also a way to prepare the community for the Lenten journey ahead. The prophet sets forth a number of actions appropriate during Lent:

- Loose the bonds of injustice
- Undo the thongs of the yoke
- Let the oppressed go free
- Share bread with the hungry
- Bring the homeless into your own home
- Clothe the naked

God will be with us, the prophet reminds us, guiding us and meeting our needs as we rebuild our lives and the lives of all those around us.

Psalm 51:1-17

The psalm appointed for Ash Wednesday also serves to prepare us for the journey. Tradition ascribes this psalm to David as his response and prayer to God after having been confronted by the prophet Nathan. It is the song and prayer of one who is willing to lay bare one's soul and admit all of one's limitations and failings.

Lent is a time to look deep into our souls. It is a time to be open and honest, not to continue to conceal our sins—from ourselves and from God. If we are willing to make the psalmist's words our words, we confess our transgressions and our sins, but we also recognize that it is only with God's help that we will be "washed clean." This will be crucial as we proceed on our Lenten journey. It is a journey in, with, and to God. It is not a time to depend solely on our ability and ourselves. We cannot put a "new and right spirit" in ourselves. It is through God's actions, not ours, that we are given new hearts and new lives. An essential dimension of our journey, therefore, is to recognize and admit our finitude.

2 Corinthians 5:20b–6:10

Paul reminds us of an important fact that is easily forgotten. We seek to be reconciled to the God who created us, and from whom we have strayed, because it is God who has first sought us and not the other way around. Writing to the new Christians in Corinth, Paul places both discipleship and penitence firmly in relationship to the incarnation. He is able to be an ambassador who endures all hardships because God became one who made the ultimate sacrifice—becoming one of us so that we might be reconciled to God.

Again we hear the call "now is the acceptable time" (2 Cor 6:2b). This will connect Paul's letter to the earlier announcements of the prophets. We are reminded that it is time to pack our bags and set off on our journey. There will be no better time. Our journey will not compare to the journey undertaken by Paul, but he provides us with a view of how it might be, as well as how we are to make it. It may be a journey of affliction, hardship, and calamity. But through all, we will persevere if we undertake the journey with purity, knowledge, and patience.

Matthew 6:1-6, 16-21

For our gospel reading we are invited to enter into the Sermon on the Mount. Jesus has been telling his followers how blessed they are to be poor in spirit, to be merciful, and pure in heart. But Jesus is also well aware that we do not always live up to that gold standard. We are not always merciful and our hearts are less than pure. How are we to give alms? How are we to pray? How are we to fast? How are we to walk the path of reconciliation?

Jesus confronts us with the question of motives. Are we giving alms because we want to care for the least? Or, are we giving alms so that others will see how generous we are and applaud our generosity? Are we praying to God or showing off for our neighbors? Jesus reminds us that, no matter how much we may fool our neighbors, we will never fool the God who sees into our very hearts.

The Gospel lesson provides a road map for our Lenten journey, inviting us to pray, fast, and give alms.

WORSHIP AND PREACHING THEMES

- Ash Wednesday is the invitation into a lengthy **preparation** for our Lenten journey. You might reflect on all of the ways that we prepare for a journey or prepare for an important change in our life such as a wedding or the birth of a baby.
- Unlike those joyful celebrations, we are preparing ourselves for **repentance**. This is a time to identify the ways that we have turned away from God, repent of those, and return. It is also a time to remind the congregation that our confession and repentance is grounded in God's love and mercy. We do not repent *so that* God will love us but rather *because* God loves us.
- **Reconciliation** between God and the people of God is, therefore, an important theme of the Ash Wednesday service. How do we come together with God? How do

we come together with friend and family and stranger alike?

- **Fasting** is an important theme of Ash Wednesday. Fasting reminds us that we are not passive, helpless individuals at the mercy of the world around us. We are able to, with God's help, take control of our lives and reject those things that hurt and harm.
- Ultimately, Ash Wednesday reminds us of our **mortality**. We are all on a journey that will end with our death—we are indeed ashes, and, one day, we will return to the earth from which we were formed. But we also declare that this is not the end but only the beginning of a journey that will last through eternity.

CREATING THE ENVIRONMENT

When will the service take place—during the day or in the evening? If the service is in the evening, the ability to darken the worship space will create an atmosphere of quiet and reflection that will not necessarily be possible for a service during daylight.

It is appropriate to create a sparse setting. There should be no flowers or bright colors. While the traditional Lenten color is purple, more and more communities are using browns and grays in rough fabrics such as burlap.

SHAPING THE WORSHIP SERVICE

Music

- "Sunday's Palms Are Wednesday's Ashes," by Rae E. Whitney
- "Lord, Who Throughout These Forty Days," by Claudia F. Hernaman
- "Give Me a Clean Heart," Margaret P. Douroux
- "Forgive Us, Lord (*Perdón, Señor*)," by Jorge Lockward

- "Out of the Depths," Ruth Duck
- "It's Me, It's Me, O Lord (Standing in the Need of Prayer)," Spiritual
- "Dust and Ashes," Brian Wren
- "I Want Jesus to Walk with Me," African American Spiritual

Opening the Service

Will the tone of the service be one of contemplation and confession? Is this a time for the congregation to reflect on its mortality; "You are dust, and to dust you shall return"? Or might your team choose to adopt the tone of Joel or Isaiah? The prophets view this as time to blow the alarm and awaken the community to its precarious situation.

Calling the Alarm

If your congregation is open to alternative ways of opening a service, you might consider asking a trumpet player to play several long, sustained notes, calling the assembly to attention. Or, in the absence of a horn player, you might have someone ring a bell loudly and vigorously.

Responsive Call to Worship

Blow the trumpet.
Sanctify a fast.
Call a solemn assembly.
**Gather the aged and the children,
even the newborn baby.**
Call God's people.
With open hearts and minds we come before God.
We come to confess our sins, our faults, our failures.
**We turn to the God who is slow to anger and abounding
in great mercy.**
Blow the trumpet and call a solemn assembly.

Entering into Contemplation

If you wish to create a quieter atmosphere, you may dim the lights of the worship space and place a number of candles throughout the space.

It will need to be light enough for people to read, but when the lights have been lowered, people will tend to be quiet as they enter for worship. You might invite musicians—perhaps a flute player, or an acoustic guitarist, to play softly as people are entering. To signal the opening of the service, you might gently ring a small bell, followed by a period of silence.

Opening Prayer

Holy and Gracious God,
Creator of all living things,
    the beginning and the end of our lives.
We gather as your people,
    ready to begin our Lenten journey.
Strengthen our hearts and minds
    through your bountiful love.
Make us ready to acknowledge
    our sins and weaknesses.
Remove our hearts of stone,
    and create in us hearts and minds
    ready to hear your words
    of forgiveness and acceptance.
This we ask in the name of the one
    who walked the way of the cross, Jesus the Christ.
Amen.

Service of the Word

The reading of the passage from Joel would work well with four readers stationed at the four corners of the worship space. The first reader would read Joel 2:1-2; and subsequent readers—Joel 2:12-14, 2:15-16, and 2:17, respectively. The reading could be opened and closed with a blast on the trumpet.

Confession and Pardon

Confession is central to the service of Ash Wednesday. There are several forms this might take. First, a more traditional prayer:

Prayer of Confession

Holy and ever loving God,
We come before you as your children,
    confessing our weaknesses
    and our failure to live a life
    worthy of your overflowing love.
We have not loved you with all
    our heart, mind, soul, and strength.
We have not loved our neighbors as ourselves.
In your great mercy, forgive us.
Create in us clean hearts and right spirits.
Help us know the joy of your saving help,
    and fill us with your Holy Spirit,
    supporting us on this our Lenten journey.
This we ask in the name of Jesus who,
    through his death on the cross
    and his resurrection, has given us everlasting life.
    Amen.

Words of Assurance and Pardon

May these ashes that will mark our foreheads be outward signs
    not only of our confession
    but also as marks of God's love and forgiveness.
Out of the dirt of the earth our God formed us,
    fashioned us, and breathed into us new life;
let us remember that we have a God
    who forgives us our sins and forgets our failings.
In the name of Christ you are forgiven.

Litany of Confession

You may also use the form of a litany for your community's confession.
Dust we are, O God, and to dust we shall return.
Have mercy on us.
We have not loved you with our whole
    heart, soul, and mind.

We have not loved our neighbors as ourselves.
We have turned away from those in need,
and squandered our inheritance with self-indulgence.
Have mercy on us.
Have mercy on us, O loving and gracious God.
Forgive us all our sins and weaknesses,
        our anger and hate.
All: We confess our prejudice and intolerance,
        our greed and envy.
We have sinned against heaven and before you;
And we are no longer worthy to be called
        your children.
But you are gracious and merciful.
Like a loving mother and father,
        welcome us back into your arms,
        that we may know your forgiveness
        and acceptance.

Words of Assurance or Pardon

(See p. 22)

Finally, you might invite people into a time of silent prayer, reflection, and confession. People may sit individually, or, if your space will allow, you might invite people to gather in smaller circles to pray silently or to speak with one another about ways that they feel they have fallen short of God's vision for them in their lives. During this time there may be silence, or you may ask a musician to play softly.

Imposition of Ashes

Open this portion of the service by lifting a large bowl of the ashes before the congregation, saying:
    In the beginning God created the heavens and the earth.
    Then the Lord God formed the human being
        from the dust of the ground,
        and breathed into its nostrils the breath of life
        and the human became a living being.

Gracious God, you have formed us from the dust;
　　　　dust we are, and to dust we shall all return.
May these ashes be a reminder that our lives
　　　　are always in your hands;
　　　　and that though we will die, yet shall we live.

The congregation will be given the opportunity to receive the ashes, in the form of a cross, on their foreheads. There are a number of ways that this might be done.

For a Small Group

If the number of those attending the service is small, you might conduct the service seated in the round. At the time in the service for the imposition of ashes, two small bowls of ashes may be sent around the circle, and each member of the group will mark the next person with the sign of the cross. This can be a very powerful experience. You may want to follow the bowl with a wet cloth so that people can clean their hands.

For a Large Group

If the number in the congregation is larger, you might have a number of small bowls of ashes that are sent down each row and the people in the row will mark the sign of the cross on the person seated next to them. Again, you might want to send a wet cloth. Or you might have several individuals come forward. They will first receive the sign of the cross themselves, and they will then, in turn, impose ashes on the remainder of the congregation as they come forward.

The Peace

As a sign of reconciliation and God's overflowing love,
　　　　Let us offer each other a sign of God's peace.
　　　　The peace of Christ be with you.
And also with you.

Closing of the Service

Whether or not you began the service with a loud trumpet alarm, it is appropriate to end this service with the silent departure of those attending. The worship leader may send the congregation out with a final blessing that includes the invitation to begin the Lenten journey.

CHAPTER THREE

FIRST SUNDAY IN LENT

TEACH US TO PRAY

While there may be members of the community who were able to participate in the worship services on Ash Wednesday, for many this will be the beginning of their Lenten journey. Therefore, in addition to the foci of the First Sunday in Lent, which are sin, the temptation to sin, and wilderness, this first Sunday must also introduce the community to the idea of, reasons for, and practices of the Lenten journey. And, if your community did not have a service on Ash Wednesday, review the prayers and worship suggestions for that service. You may be able to incorporate some of those worship plans into your service for the First Sunday in Lent.

Luke tells us that, as Jesus made his journey to Jerusalem, the disciples asked their teacher, "Teach us to pray." Recorded in both Matthew and Luke we read the answer to that question. It is what we have come to call the Lord's Prayer. We are to pray not to a distant God but to a God that we are to address as our loving parent. With that sense of intimacy and openness, we are to ask for bread, our most basic need of sustenance. We are to ask for forgiveness from our parent God as we forgive those who wrong us. And we are to pray that we will not be brought "to the time of trial" (Luke 11:4b), with Matthew adding the plea, "but rescue us from the evil one" (Matt 6:13b).

The First Sunday in Lent is, in many ways, an opportunity to begin our journey by reflecting on those themes present in the Lord's Prayer. The Gospel lessons in all three Lectionary years tell the story of Jesus' experience in the wilderness, when he not only prayed to God, whom he called *Abba*, but when he was brought to a time of trial and was confronted by the evil one.

During Lent we too will explore our temptations. We will reflect on where we have fallen short and succumbed, confessing our weaknesses. And we will draw strength and direction for the journey from the one who has journeyed ahead of us.

SITTING WITH THE TEXT

Year A

Genesis 2:15-17; 3:1-17

Those inside and outside the church alike know the story of the tree, the apple (that really isn't an apple), the serpent, and the errant Eve and Adam. From paintings to cartoons, most everyone knows the story. Or at least, they *think* they know the story. This is an excellent time to look beyond the stereotypes and examine the meaning of this foundational text. It is much more than a weak woman leading the man astray.

The theme of temptation appears in both the Old Testament lesson and in the Gospel lesson. Eve was tempted. Jesus was tempted. The difference lies in Eve's succumbing to the "fast-talking" serpent that offers wisdom and knowledge to her. Adam and Eve are presented with a choice. They may continue to live into the life that God has envisioned for them, or they may seek to walk their own path. The reality is that we too are tempted each and every day. Where are you being tempted?

Psalm 32

This penitential psalm offers us an excellent pattern for our Lenten prayers and reflections. While the psalmist admits to having fallen short, that is not where the psalm begins. It begins with the acknowledgment that God will forgive our sins. It is in the light of this good news that we are able to confess our faults.

The psalmist presents us with a telling portrait of what it means to hide our sins; when silent, "my body wasted away," and "my strength was dried up" (Ps 32:3, 4). Many have come to realize the connection between our spiritual and physical state. Lent is an opportunity to reflect on that connection and our call to be honest with God and with ourselves.

Romans 5:12-19

The reading from Paul's letter to the people in Rome examines the relationship between the "first" Adam, and the "second," Jesus. How was it that sin came into the world? Through Adam (and Eve), sin came into the world, and through the "free gift" of Jesus, we have been given the way to "justification and life."

You might wish to examine paintings and icons of the crucifixion. Frequently, the cross is placed on a slight rise. Underneath the cross is a skull and bones. Early in the church, the story circulated that the cross had been placed above the grave of Adam—giving us a visual representation of Paul's preaching.

Matthew 4:1-11

Jesus has been baptized and is directed into the wilderness by the Holy Spirit in order to be tempted by the devil. As in Genesis, the tempter asks questions. The serpent did not direct Eve to eat the fruit of the tree; rather, it asked her to tell it God's instructions. Likewise, the tempter is not so much interested in seeing Jesus do "tricks" as he is in discovering who Jesus is and whether or not Jesus will turn away from God.

The devil wants to know if Jesus is the Son of God. We know that Jesus is the Son, having "heard" the voice of God at Jesus' baptism, "This is my Son, the Beloved" (Matt 3:17). With this knowledge we can be confident as we pick up our cross and follow. We watch Jesus stand up to the tempter and we learn

from him. Unlike Eve and Adam, he is able to resist the temptations to forsake God and follow the devil. Worldly pleasures and
powers are not the way of the cross. The way of the cross calls for
trusting and worshiping the one true God.

Year B

Genesis 9:8-17

The ark has been built and filled, and the water has come and
gone. In this reading, it is God who declares to Noah that,
because of his faithfulness, God will "establish a covenant" of life.
God will never again will a flood to destroy all living things on
the earth.

As with the story of Adam and Eve in Year A, this is a reading
that many people *think* they know. While there does not seem to
be a direct connection between the story of Noah and Jesus'
temptation in the wilderness, it is a story of God's call and the
need to be faithful in the voyage into a watery wilderness.

As you study this text, you might benefit from reading the
entire story of Noah—Genesis 6–9. More than the folk art repre-
sentations of a boat filled with sweet animals, this is the story of
sin and its painful consequences. We do well to remember that
outside of Noah, his family, and a remnant of the earth's animals
and birds, all other living creatures were destroyed. Rather than
looking at paintings of Noah and the ark, your reflections might
be aided by reviewing pictures of the terrible destruction of the
Tsunami in 2004, Hurricanes Katrina and Rita in 2005, or the
devastation in 2008 from the cyclone in Myanmar and the earth-
quake in China.

Psalm 25:1-10

As the community of God sets off on its Lenten journey, it
turns to the words of the psalmist, who reminds us that the way
of the Lord is a path of truth, salvation, mercy, love, and faithfulness. It echoes the reading from Genesis, grounding the journey

toward God in God's covenant. We are able to be faithful because God is first faithful.

1 Peter 3:18-22

When reading passages of Scripture, it is always important to step back and consider the larger picture. That is certainly important in this reading of the first letter of Peter. The epistle reading presents the reader with a richness of images: Noah and those who were saved from the flood, the suffering of Jesus on the cross, the resurrections, heaven, and angels. The call for a good conscience may connect this reading to the others. The writer wants to help new Christians—born anew through baptism—understand what their new life, "as aliens and exiles" (1 Pet 2:11), should be like.

Do we think of ourselves as aliens or exiles? What would our lives be like if we did?

Mark 1:9-15

Peter writes to the new Christians that their baptism has put them at odds with the culture in which they live. Mark's account of Jesus' testing in the wilderness would seem to indicate that Jesus' baptism put him at odds with God. No sooner had Jesus heard the declaration, "You are my Son, the Beloved; with you I am well pleased," than we are told that the Holy Spirit "drove" him into the wilderness. The Greek word *ekballō* is the same word used when the people of Nazareth seek to "drive" Jesus out of town, and when Jesus "drives" the moneychangers out of the temple.

In the wilderness Jesus is tested for the mission and task that lie ahead of him. Mark tells us little more than the fact that Satan tempts Jesus. But he offers the intriguing image of Jesus being surrounded by angels and wild animals. Jesus is protected from the animals and sustained by the ministrations of the angels for forty days. We are to be reminded of the flood, the Israelites' wandering in the wilderness, and Elijah's flight into the wilderness.

Where do we find ourselves as we enter our Lenten journey? Are we in the wilderness?

Year C

Deuteronomy 26:1-11

The opening scripture is a call to remember all that God has done for God's people and to respond by giving God our best—the first fruits. Throughout Lent, the readings from the Old Testament will tell the story of God's abundant love, focusing on the Passover and the freeing of the children of Israel. They are to remember what God has done for them, bringing them release from captivity and giving them a place, the land in which they will flourish. They are to remember and they are to respond with thankfulness.

The sense of being led by God may be a connecting point with the Gospel lesson. There we read that the Holy Spirit led Jesus into the wilderness.

Psalm 91:1-2, 9-16

In the Gospel lesson, the devil will challenge Jesus to throw himself off the highest point of the temple, trusting that God will save him because God's angels will not let anything happen to him. Jesus is not the only one who quotes Scripture; the devil is quoting Psalm 91.

It is difficult to read this psalm without shaking one's head at the supreme confidence voiced by the psalmist. We are right to put our trust in God who is our "refuge and fortress." But we would be foolish to think that God will allow us to stomp on the foot of a lion or the head of a rattlesnake. God is with us in times of trouble, but as the events of the Passion will demonstrate, faith in God does not make us invulnerable. Nevertheless, the psalmist reminds us that, whenever we call for God, God is there and God will answer.

Romans 10:8b-13

As we move into our Lenten journey, we do well to travel with Paul's reassurance that, "Everyone who calls on the name of the Lord shall be saved" (Romans 10:13). We are comforted by the knowledge that we have been saved. It is not a journey to find Christ. Paul reminds us that we have already been found by Christ—the Word is near when we confess our faith and proclaim the good news.

Luke 4:1-13

The Holy Spirit plays, for Luke, a central role in the gospel story. Jesus' birth comes about by the power of the Holy Spirit. At his baptism, the Holy Spirit descends upon Jesus like a dove. Jesus, John the Baptizer declares, is coming to baptize us with the Holy Spirit and fire. And it is both filled with and led by the Holy Spirit that Jesus journeys into the wilderness to be tested by the devil. It is not clear from the text whether the period of temptation is the entire forty days or comes only at the end. Notice that the three temptations reported by Luke do come at the end of the forty days.

Filled with the Holy Spirit, Jesus is able to confront and, for the time being, defeat the devil. The devil wants to know who Jesus is and the devil is looking for signs. The Son of God would be able to turn stones into bread and plunge from the tower of the temple unscathed. But those are not the signs by which he will be recognized. Later, when the disciples of John ask Jesus the same question, he directs their attention to the fruits of his labors: the blind see, the lame walk, leapers are cleansed, the deaf hear, and the dead are raised.

The devil quotes Scripture (Psalm 91), and Jesus responds by quoting from Deuteronomy (8:3, then 6:13 and 6:16). We are, Jesus tells us, not to test God but are to live by the Word of God, to worship God, and to serve only God. Those, perhaps, are excellent guides for our Lenten journey.

WORSHIP AND PREACHING THEMES

- **Wilderness** is a significant theme. Clearly it is a location or place—the Israelites wandered in the wilderness for forty years. Jesus was driven or led into a particular place. But that place is significant symbolically as well. Wilderness is a place, or time, of hardship and loneliness. It is wherever and whenever people confront the edge of life, where temptation and death prowl in the shadows. Wilderness can also be places or experiences that bring clarity and enlightenment to individuals or communities.

- The theme of **temptation** and **testing** might be explored. These are certainly appropriate themes for the start of the Lenten journey. The argument might be advanced that there is nothing wrong with being tempted. What is in question is how we respond to that testing. Are we able to resist the temptations that surround us, or do we succumb to their pull? What do temptations look like? How do we recognize them? How did Jesus know that it was a sin to turn stones into bread?

- You may wish to explore the theological understanding of **sin.** What happens when we give in to temptation and fail the test? What does sin do to our relationship to God and to others? What does sin do to our understanding of our self?

- The Scriptures ask us to **remember.** As we move forward on our Lenten journey, we need to look back as well. We need to remember what God has done for us in the past. We need to remember the ways that we have been tested before, the ways we have cried to God. And we must remember the ways that God has heard our calls and answered us.

- Finally, you might focus on **faithfulness** and **trust.** Jesus was faithful to God and would not worship the devil. He trusted that God would care for him. Noah was faithful and trusted that God would save him. Eve and Adam did not trust God. They gave in to the temptation to gain more knowledge and wisdom. They wanted to be in charge of their lives. Are we faithful? Do we trust that God has our best interests at heart? Or, are we stiff-necked and obstinate?

CREATING THE ENVIRONMENT

Large clear glass vases filled with bare branches might suggest the barrenness of the wilderness. If you fill the vases with sand, it will hold the branches as well as serving as a visual reminder of the wasteland. You might also place large rocks near the bases. If you are able to project images, you might use desert landscapes.

SHAPING THE WORSHIP SERVICE

As was noted at the opening of this chapter, for many people this will be the start of their Lenten journey. This service, therefore, must perform two functions. First, it will explore the lessons and themes of the First Sunday of Lent: wilderness, temptation, sin, remembrance, and faithfulness. But it must also preview the entire Lenten journey toward the Passion. This is the congregation's opportunity to reflect on the Lenten disciplines of Bible study, fasting, giving alms, and service.

Music

- "Guide Me, O Thou Great Jehovah," by William Williams
- "Will You Come and Follow Me?" by John Bell
- "Lord, Who Throughout These Forty Days," by Claudia F. Hernaman
- "Lead Me, Guide Me," by Doris Akers

- "Trust and Obey," by John H. Sammis
- "Good to Me," by Craig Musseau
- "Praise Him! Jesus, Blessed Savior," by Donnie Harper
- "Change My Heart, O God," by Eddie Espinosa
- "I Will Trust in the Lord," African American Spiritual

Opening the Service

Responsive Call to Worship (based on Psalms 25 and 91)

To you, O God, we lift our souls.
You are our refuge and our fortress,
    in you we place our trust.
Lead us in the ways of righteousness and truth,
Save us from the time of trial.
Make us to know your ways, O Holy One;
All the paths of God are steadfast love and faithfulness,
        for those who keep God's covenant and decrees,
        help us as we begin to walk the way of the cross.

Opening Prayer

Holy God, loving creator, giver of all life;
like Jesus, we find ourselves in the wilderness of life,
        tempted to turn from you and your love.
Fill us with your Holy Spirit
        that we may face the assaults of the enemy.
Strengthen us and help us
        walk the path you set before us.
All this we ask in the name of the faithful one, Jesus.
Amen.

Welcoming Those to Be Baptized

If you have a group of people who are preparing to be baptized at the Easter Vigil, the First Sunday in Lent may be an appropriate time to present them to the community. Invite the community to pray for them during Lent, and ask the community to be available to answer their questions during this time of preparation.

(Call forward those in preparation for baptism.)
Dear sisters and brothers in Christ. We present to you (*read names*), who are preparing for baptism at the Easter Vigil. As we prepare to welcome them to the body of Christ and to our community, may we support them in this journey. Let us pray together:

Holy God, be with these your children, as they prepare to go down into the waters of baptism. Strengthen and support them, and be with us as we walk this journey with them. Send your Holy Spirit to be with all of us on our Lenten journey that we may, at the end of our journey, celebrate with joy the new life we have been given through the death and resurrection of your Son, our savior, Jesus Christ. Amen.

Service of the Word

The readings for Years A and C lend themselves to a dramatic reading. You might consider a choral reading of the confrontation between Jesus and the tempter. While individuals might read the parts of Jesus and the narrator, have several people, perhaps four or five people, read the part of the tempter. Place the persons reading the parts of the narrator and Jesus at the front of the worship space, but place those reading the part of the tempter around the worship space so that they are surrounding the worshipers, just as the tempter surrounds us.

A Reading Adapted from Matthew 4:1-11

Narrator: Then Jesus was led up by the Spirit into the wilderness to be tempted by the devil. He fasted forty days and forty nights, and afterwards he was famished. The tempter came and said to him,

Tempter: If you are the Son of God, command these stones to become loaves of bread.

Narrator: But Jesus answered,
   Jesus: It is written,
"One does not live by bread alone,
but by every word that comes from the mouth
of God."
Narrator: Then the devil took Jesus to the holy city and
placed him on the pinnacle of the temple, say-
ing to him,
Tempter: If you are the Son of God, throw yourself down;
for it is written,
"He will command his angels concerning you.
On their hands they will bear you up,
so that you will not dash your foot against a
stone."
Narrator: Jesus said to the tempter,
   Jesus: Again it is written,
"Do not put the Lord your God to the test."
Narrator: The devil took Jesus to a very high mountain
and showed him all the kingdoms of the world
and their splendor; then the tempter said to Jesus,
Tempter: All these I will give you, if you will fall down
and worship me.
Narrator: But Jesus said to the devil,
   Jesus: Away with you, Satan! For it is written,
"Worship the Lord your God, and serve only
[God]."
Narrator: Then the devil left Jesus, and suddenly angels
came and waited on him.

Confession and Pardon

Prayer of Confession

We come before you, O God, your wayward children.
We confess to you our love of worldly goods.
We prefer to live by bread alone rather than
    your life-giving Word.

We confess to you that we do not trust in
    your saving love.
We test and question your presence in our lives.
We do not see your angels that surround us.
We confess to you that we worship
    worldly power and success.
We ignore those in need.
We believe that it is we, rather than you,
    who has charge over the world.
Forgive us our sins and weakness,
    and set us on the path toward health and wholeness
    that can be found only in you.
May we worship and serve only you,
    now and forever. Amen.

Words of Assurance and Pardon

As we walk this Lenten journey,
    we do so with the God of love.
Our God accepts us when we turn away from sin
    and turn toward new life in God.
Through the power of the Holy Spirit
    may you grow in grace.

Dismissal

Go now, filled with the love and spirit of the God who
    has given us new life.
Walk the way of the cross.
Be strong in the face of temptation,
Bring the good news that the reign of God has come near.
Grace and peace be with you all.

CHAPTER FOUR

SECOND SUNDAY IN LENT

FOLLOW ME

Follow me, Jesus tells us. But have you ever tried to follow someone when you don't know where you are going? Do you know what it means to be lost?

When my ninety-eight-year-old grandmother died, the family gathered for her funeral. As we were heading to our cars to make the drive from the church to the cemetery, the funeral director instructed us to turn on our lights and flashers, and said, "Just follow me." Unfortunately, what he did not give us were maps, nor did he drive slowly. He took off like a flash and soon many of us were wandering around the city, trying to find our way. It was the worst kind of "lost" we had ever experienced. We were afraid that we would miss our grandmother's burial. Fortunately, both my mother and I had our cell phones, and like a control tower to a pilot, she guided us through the city to the cemetery.

Follow me. The theme of the Second Sunday in Lent is God's call to follow, to radically change our lives. We read the story of our father in the faith, Abraham. We remember the startling call to leave behind his home, his family. We reflect on the faith that is needed to trust in God, and as Jesus commands us, to pick up our cross and follow the one who leads the way.

The Second Sunday in Lent is a moment in our journey to ask ourselves—when have we heard God's call? What has God called us to do? How have we answered God's call and changed our lives? Or, how do we turn away, ignoring that call?

SITTING WITH THE TEXT

Year A

Genesis 12:1-4a

This portion of Genesis is foundational for three of the world's major religions—Judaism, Christianity, and Islam—the Abrahamic faiths. It records that pivotal moment when God speaks to Abram, calling him to leave his home and his family, promising that out of Abram, God will make a great nation. There is no warning, no reason given. All we know about Abram is that he is the son of Terah, a descendant of Noah's son Shem, and that he is married to a woman named Sarai. What is Abram like? Why does God call him? Has he done anything special? Is he a particularly holy man? We were told that Noah found favor in the sight of God, but of Abram we know nothing.

This is the moment of transition from the primeval history to the story of the Patriarchs, and it begins the story of salvation of which we are still a part. It is our story, for we are the children of Abraham and Sarah, the people who answered God's call.

We should notice that Abram is silent. He does not ask God any questions. He does not bargain or barter; he does not seem to ask why God is making this unusual command. He simply picks up his family and his belongings, and "went, as the LORD had told him." Do we have the same response to God's call in our lives? Or, do we have the "just a minute" or "let me finish this" response?

Finally, we should notice that this is not a call to a metaphorical journey such as the one that we have undertaken during

Lent. This is about a real journey, about a real land, about a real family and people that Abram and Sarai are to leave behind. Think of the times you have left behind the known and familiar, and ventured into a new place. It is very unsettling and frightening to begin a new life in a new place.

Psalm 121

Throughout the Psalter are those songs identified as "Psalms of Ascent." They are the songs that pilgrims sang as they traveled to Jerusalem for religious festivals and temple duties. Psalm 121 is one such song. While we are inclined to read this psalm from a metaphorical point of view—most of us are not really looking up into hills—those traveling to Jerusalem are setting off on a potentially perilous journey. Who will protect them? Who will be their "keeper," and keep them from "all evil?" It is God, of course, the God who has called them to follow. God is with them from the start of their journey until the end. Day and night God watches over them.

As we travel on our Lenten journey, answering God's call, we too are called to lift our eyes to the hills and see that God is with us every step of the way. Enter into the psalm and reflect on the portrait of God painted by the psalmist. How and when have you experienced God's faithfulness and constancy in your life?

Romans 4:1-5, 13-17

As Paul tries to explain to the new Christians in Rome, the free gift of justification and new life that God has given us in and through the death and resurrection of Jesus Christ, he turns to the example of Abraham. Abraham, he argues, did not work for or earn the promise that he would "inherit the world." Abraham is our "father" in the faith because of his own faith. He believed God, "and it was reckoned to him as righteousness" (Rom 4:3).

The challenge as we read these passages is to focus on the good news of God's grace and not to fall into the trap of thinking that its only message is that Judaism and the law are bad and

Christianity and grace are good. To do so is to seriously derail our Lenten journey.

John 3:1-17

There are two possible Gospel lessons for the Second Sunday. The first invites us in to eavesdrop on the encounter between Jesus and Nicodemus. Nicodemus, a wise and respected leader, has been watching what Jesus has been doing, and he is trying to make sense of who this person Jesus is and what he is doing. Like many of us, it may be that Nicodemus wants to be in control of his life and follow a predictable path.

The important message of Jesus, here in the opening chapters of John's Gospel, is that the path Jesus is going to follow (the path he is asking us to follow) is far from predictable. He talks about being born anew, being born from above. Who can control how or when one is born? Jesus reminds Nicodemus that the Spirit of God is like a wind that we cannot control.

Throughout our Lenten journey we are invited to enter into reflection on the strange and mysterious ways of God. It is only through the Spirit and grace of God that filled the lives of Abraham and Sarah, those pilgrims on the road to Jerusalem, and Paul, that we are blown into new ways of living in God's reign. And it is through the Son, who will be lifted up, that we have the gift of eternal life.

Matthew 17:1-9

The optional Gospel reading is the story of the Transfiguration. Jesus has called Peter, James, and John up on the mountain with him. Mountains have often been places of divine encounter and revelation, and once more the people of God encounter the awesome and the confusing. While they think that they know and understand the person whom they have been following, their beloved teacher, suddenly they are given a glimpse of Jesus' full glory.

To read the story of the Transfiguration is to be given a glimpse of what is possible through God's love and grace. It is a vision that will comfort the disciples, and can comfort us in the dark days of Holy Week.

Year B

Genesis 17:1-7, 15-16

Much has happened in the life journey of Abram and Sarai since they left their homeland and family at God's call. But God's promise seems not to have been fulfilled. God had called them to follow and would make of them a great nation. But how can they be the parents of future generations, if they have no children?

In the reading for the Second Sunday we hear God's promise again. And what a foolish promise it seems to be. Abram and Sarai are now ancient, far beyond the age of bearing children, and yet this "foolish" God declares the good news of a covenant between God and these faithful servants. They are given new names and the assurance that they will have a son.

Of course, we know the rest of the story. We know that God keeps this promise. We know that, with God, all things are possible, even giving birth in one's old age. But we must remember that Abram is again walking by faith. He does not really know that this will indeed come to pass. What difference does it make to be given a new name? Can God make of an old woman and an old man the ancestor of a "multitude of nations"? What impossible things might God be doing in your lives?

Psalm 22:23-31

The psalm picks up the image of family. What does it mean to think of all people as part of the family of God? The psalmist declares that those who worship God are not limited to a small group of desert people, but that all nations will bow down. Nor is worship limited by time and place. God promised Abraham that he had a future, and that his descendents had a future within God's care; the psalmist declares that the future of all generations is in God's hands.

Romans 4:13-25

Who are we able to claim as our parents or grandparents? How is it that Paul is able to claim that even those who were not born under the law might call Abraham their father? To whose family do we all belong? We are given life; we are made one family through the grace and love of God.

Paul holds up a portrait of a God who is faithful and who keeps promises. He wants us to reflect upon all of the new and startling things that God has done and continues to do. It was God who made of Abraham a great nation and it was God who brought Jesus Christ out of death into life. Do we watch for all of the new things that God continues to do?

Mark 8:31-38

In the First Sunday in Lent, we encountered Satan tempting Jesus to stray from the path on which God had set him. This week we seem to encounter Satan in another guise. This time it is Peter, Jesus' faithful friend, who tempts Jesus to stray.

Jesus had asked the disciples to tell him who they thought that he was. Peter enthusiastically gives the audacious answer that Jesus is the Messiah for whom all have been waiting. But does he really know what he is saying? Jesus thinks not.

To be the Messiah, Jesus tells them, to be God's anointed chosen one, doesn't mean fame and glory, rather, it means that he will be rejected and killed. While Jesus tells them that he will rise again, Peter focuses only on the bad news, the message of failure and death. And again, Jesus rejects the tempter, "Get behind me, Satan!" Peter, Jesus explains, is thinking in the world's terms, not God's. The call of Jesus is not to fame but to join him in the walk toward the cross. It is not about becoming rich and successful in the eyes of the world. That might mean that we lose our lives. The way to save our lives is to lose them in the love of God.

As we continue on our Lenten journey, what are those things that tempt us off the path? How are we thinking in worldly ways?

Mark 9:2-9

An alternative Gospel is Mark's account of the Transfiguration. See the discussion in Year A.

Year C

Genesis 15:1-12, 17-18

"Promises, promises," says Abram, complaining to God. "You tell me one thing, but my life seems to say another. You tell me that I am going to be the father of a great nation, but I don't see any children running around my table. How can I believe what you tell me?" What does it mean, he seems to wonder, to answer God's call and step out into the unknown? Can we trust God to deliver? Will God come through in the end?

If we look at the twelfth chapter of Genesis, we see that, when God called Abram to leave his home and his family, Abram did so without question or challenge. Like Paul, we lift up Abraham as the faithful founder of our family. Through his faith and trust in God and by stepping out in faith, he was justified and found righteous by God. How can we think that we might be able to live up to that unquestioning faith? This moment in the life of Abram and Sarai gives us hope. He did question. He did wonder if what God said was true.

As we walk faith's journey, we may encounter those moments in our lives that cause us to question and doubt. The good news is that God did not reject and dismiss Abram. Rather, God was gentle and understanding. Abram asked for a sign and a sign was given to him. For Abram, the sign that he was following the right path and that God would keep the covenant was a smoking fire pot and flaming torch.

During our Lenten journey, God will not ask us to sacrifice a ram, turtledove, or young pigeon. But, by keeping our Lenten disciplines of Bible study, fasting, giving alms, and service, we will be joined by our God who is faithful and loving. We will not lose our way and we always have before us our sign of God's love—Jesus Christ.

Psalm 27

The scriptures do not tell us that, if we follow the right path toward the God who has called us, our lives will be trouble free. We will encounter adversaries and adversities. Yet through all that, the psalmist reminds us, we are never alone. God is our "light and salvation." A goal of our Lenten experience, therefore, is to train the sight of our spirit to watch for and to be attentive to "see the goodness of the LORD."

Philippians 3:17–4:1

While many of us try to model our lives after Jesus, picking up our crosses and following him, we also know that it helps to have people around us who give us an idea of what the faithful life will look like. We know that we will never be able to live up to the sacrifice made by Christ. It seems rather forward of Paul to tell us that we should imitate him. We may identify people as saints of God, but we are suspicious when someone declares her or himself to be a saint.

What is it about his life that Paul thinks we should imitate? He encourages us to keep our eyes fixed on the cross of Christ. We are to be like Paul and remember that we have been made, through our baptism, citizens of heaven. We may live on the earth, but there are many things and many people on earth that will seek to sway us from the right path. "Stand firm in the Lord," he reminds us, and we will see our reward.

Luke 13:31-35

Self-preservation seems to be built into our very makeup. So, if someone warns us that we are in danger, we are most likely to heed that warning and get out of harm's way. Jesus has set his face toward Jerusalem and will let nothing pull him away from what awaits him. In fact, when he is warned that he is in danger, he declares that he will continue to do what he is doing. Jesus will continue to heal the sick and care for the people of God, even if that means that Herod succeeds in killing him.

We hear Jesus' steadfastness, and we hear his foreshadowing of the events that must unfold. We also hear his compassion and distress. He would like to save and comfort us from what lies ahead, but we will not listen.

For Jesus, Jerusalem was the goal and end. What is our end? Are we listening, or do we ignore the word of Jesus who seeks to protect us?

Luke 9:28-36

Luke's recounting of the Transfiguration is an alternate Gospel lesson. You may refer to the earlier discussion in Year A.

WORSHIP AND PREACHING THEMES

- Throughout the lessons for this Second Sunday is the theme of God's **call** to us to **follow**. From the call to Abram to Jesus' call to "take up [our] cross and follow" him (Mark 8:34). We are reminded that it is God who has acted first. We have not gone seeking God; God has called us. We are responding to God's **invitation**.
- God's **promises** to us are a significant theme. God promises Abraham and Sarah that they will be the parents of a great nation. We are their children and the proof that God is faithful and keeps those promises. You might explore the promises that God has made throughout salvation history and God's faithfulness.
- An important dimension of responding to God's call and invitation is **trust**. In Abraham and in Paul we have been given glimpses of what it means to trust in God. If you did not explore trust in the previous week, you might do that at this point.
- Abram is commanded to leave behind his home and his family—the known and familiar. Jesus reminds Nicodemus that one must be born anew. **Risk** and the **unknown** are important themes. When we set out into

life in God; when we follow this path, we do not always know what or who we will encounter.

CREATING THE ENVIRONMENT

If you choose to explore the theme of call and following God's path, you might cover the walls leading into the church with large maps. You might also place footprints on the floor throughout the church.

SHAPING THE WORSHIP SERVICE

Music

- "Where He Leads Me," by E. W. Blandy
- "Take Up Thy Cross," by Charles W. Everest
- "This Is the Day of New Beginnings," by Brian Wren
- "O Spirit of the Living God," by Henry H. Tweedy
- "We Walk by Faith," by Henry Alford
- "Lift High the Cross," by George William Kitchin and Michael Robert Newbolt
- "We Are Called (Come! Live in the Light!)," by David Haas
- "Will You Come and Follow Me (The Summons)," by John Bell
- "I Want Jesus to Walk with Me," African American Spiritual
- "On Eagle's Wings," by Michael Joncas

Opening the Service

Call to Worship

As travelers on the journey of faith, God has called us.
Our help comes from the Lord.

Out of country and family, God has called us.
Our help comes from the Lord.
Filled with the Spirit, we have been born into a new life.
Our help comes from the Lord.
Pick up your cross, we hear our savior say.
We pick up our crosses, and follow—
> **for our help comes from the Lord**
> **who has called us.**

Opening Prayer

Holy and gracious God, we come as your children, more numerous than the stars in the heavens. We long to hear your voice for we are filled with uncertainty and confusion. Be with us and fill us with your Spirit. Give us the strength to answer your call to new life in Christ our Lord. **Amen.**

Service of the Word

We often forget that the psalms are songs. We may sing the response, but Lent may be an opportunity to engage the congregation in choral reading. This will take some introductory instructions. Divide your congregation in half. One-half of the congregation will read the odd-numbered verses while the other half will read the even. The key will be to have them turn and face one another as they read. This will help them understand that the psalms, in addition to being songs, are dialogues. They are the people of God speaking to, encouraging, and challenging one another.

Confession and Pardon

Litany of Confession

Left side: Holy God, you have given us the gift of new life.
Right side: You are faithful, keeping the promises that you have made to us.

49

Left side: Yet we turn away from you.
Right side: We follow another path.
Left side: We set our minds on earthly things,
Right side: and we live as enemies of the cross.
Left side: Fill us with your Spirit,
Right side: that we may answer your call to us.
Left side: Set our feet on the path toward you.
Right side: Help us stand firm in the Lord.
All: Thanks be to you, O God, who has not forsaken us.

Words of Assurance

One: Our help comes from the Lord. Our loving God will keep us from all evil. Our God will keep our going out and our coming in. In the name of God, you are forgiven.
All: In the name of God, you are forgiven. Thanks be to God.

Closing Prayer

Gracious God, you have called us to out of the old and into our new life in Christ. We have begun our Lenten journeys. Be with us this day and every day, as we face the turmoil and tumult of this life. Help us stand firm against the temptations of the tempter and help us hold fast to the promises that we have made. These we ask in the name of the risen one who has brought us new life, Jesus the Christ.

CHAPTER FIVE

THIRD SUNDAY IN LENT

I THIRST

When the community gathers at the foot of the cross on Good Friday, we will hear Jesus declare, "I thirst." For what did he thirst: for water, for justice, for an end to his suffering, for our faithfulness? True physical thirst is something that most of us in North America rarely experience. In fact, our landfills are being overrun by the small plastic water bottles that are now everywhere.

While we may rarely thirst for something to satisfy our physical needs, a significant theme of this Third Sunday in Lent is our never-ending thirst for gratification. We always want our physical needs met. We thirst for food, drink, fame, and fortune. We thirst for certainty in our lives, and we thirst for knowledge of who God is and what God is doing in our lives.

Unfortunately, as God's grace fills our lives, we hunger for the next gift and the next. I am reminded of my son on his birthday when he was young. As he sat surrounded by the opened gifts, he looked up at us and asked, "Is this all?" Thanks be to God who is gracious and merciful and forgives us our sins when we ask, "Is this all?" I am glad that God does not respond the way I was tempted to respond to my son's question.

Our Lenten journey is a fitting time to reflect on those things for which we thirst and that turn us away from God. It is also a time to identify the thirsts that are appropriate: a thirst for God, for justice, for love, and for compassion.

SITTING WITH THE TEXT

Year A

Exodus 17:1-7

How quickly we forget all that God has done for us! God has rescued the children of Israel from bondage in Egypt. God has seen them safely through the waters of the Red Sea, out of the hands of the soldiers of Pharaoh, and still they complain. In all the gifts we have been given by God at our creation, a long memory is apparently not one of them.

Like most of us, the people of Israel are thinking with their bellies. But is their request unreasonable? Might not we all worry if we found ourselves in the middle of the desert without food or water? So, as soon as their physical needs are not immediately met, they turn on Moses. They are thirsty and afraid they are going to die. They are wondering where God is and why they ever left the safety and security they had in Egypt, apparently forgetting their servitude.

Moses quickly reminds them that he is not in charge. It was not Moses who led them out of slavery but God. And in the end, it is not the leadership skills of Moses that will keep them from death but God's never-failing love and care. He reminds them that they are not quarreling with him, but they are testing and questioning the God who has called them to this new life. The journey is about faith and trust.

This lesson is about God's faithfulness in spite of our faithlessness. The people tested God and still God met their needs. When Moses followed God's instructions and struck the rock at Horeb, water gushed forth. Yet it is not God's graciousness that Moses remembered as he named the place. He named it Massah and

Meribah. Going forward, future generations would be reminded that it was there that the children of Israel *quarreled* with and *tested* God. What is the character of our journey? Are we thankful and trusting, or do we quarrel and test? Do we focus on what we have or what we do not have?

Psalm 95

The connection between this psalm and the passage from Exodus is obviously the reference to Massah and Meribah. Future generations did, in fact, remember that the people in the wilderness had quarreled with and tested God. The psalm is a call to put one's trust in the God "who's got the whole world in his hands." And this psalm counters the image of the "watchmaker" God. Our God, who is above all other gods, did not create the world and just let it run on its own. God made the sea and the dry land, but even now, even today, "In [God's] hand are the depths of the earth" and the "heights of the mountains."

The psalm is calling us to listen. The people in the wilderness hardened their hearts and refused to acknowledge God's presence in their lives. Do we hear God calling us, or do we, with hardened hearts, hear rather the siren call of other gods—fame, fortune, power, success, instant gratification?

You might reflect on the image of God as the rock that appears in both Exodus and the psalm. A rock can be something that seems to get in our way as well as a firm foundation.

Romans 5:1-11

If the passage in Exodus paints a portrait of the people of God who are whining and complaining, Paul puts before us the call to be a people who are sure and confident in God's love and mercy. We, he declares, who have been justified by faith and have found the peace of God through the death and resurrection of Jesus Christ, will be able to handle all that life will bring.

When we are in the middle of suffering, a wilderness moment, it is difficult to see how this is "a good thing." Yet how many times have we looked back on those challenging moments in our lives and realized that, with God's help and support, we did, as Paul observes, grow in character. Paul wants us to appreciate God's presence through the journey. It is in God that we have reason to hope.

As we reflect on Paul's message, it is important to direct our focus to God's faithfulness and love. We must be careful that we don't see this as a call to suffer needlessly. Unfortunately, this passage has all too often been used to keep people in an unjust situation with the mistaken belief that their suffering is good.

John 4:5-42

Although she is unnamed, the story of this Samaritan woman is central in the Gospels. It is the longest conversation between Jesus and an individual in all the New Testament. The woman has come to the town's well to meet her physical need for water, but in the end it is her spiritual thirst for new life that is met. And it is this unnamed woman who becomes the first evangelist. John tells us that many believed because of what she told them about Jesus.

The Gospel passage is a call to see life in new ways. We are to have a new way of understanding God's presence in our lives—the word has been made flesh. We are to have a new way of worshiping God—not in the temple or on the mountain, but in spirit and in truth. We are to thirst, not for water from the well, but for the living water that is God.

This is a rich text and offers a number of different preaching and worship themes. It connects with the passage from Exodus in the play on the image of water and thirst. The conversation is marked by misunderstanding and various uses of the word *water*. The woman thinks only in terms of actual water—missing the gift of God that is standing before her.

You may also explore the meaning of Jesus speaking to a woman in Samaria. This raises the theme of the good news extending beyond the children of Israel. It also examines the fact that Jesus would speak to the outcast.

We might also explore the trust that the woman came to have in Jesus. At first she was suspicious. She is then confused. She seems to think that he will build her an aqueduct to deliver water directly into her home—Jesus as plumber. But she is willing to trust him and finally comes to appreciate the good news he is preaching. The experience of this unnamed woman reminds us that only God will fill the deepest thirsts of our lives.

Year B

Exodus 20:1-17

This text from Exodus could be easily given a title—"The Ten Commandments." It might equally be dismissed as the "thou shalts and shalt nots" we don't want to hear. But what happens to a community when it enters into reflection on the law, not as something that binds us but rather as that which gives us perfect freedom?

We always seem to get the order wrong. We think that these are the "rules" that we are to follow that will win us God's love and favor. But look at the opening of the passage—"I am the LORD your God, who brought you out of the land of Egypt, out of the house of slavery" (Exod 20:2). Think about what God has already done for the children of Israel. They have been given freedom and a new life. It is in that new life and in this well-established relationship with God that they are given the law to help shape that new life.

The focus of the law is, as Jesus reminds us, that we love God with all our heart, mind, soul, and strength. When we enter into this relationship with God, it is exclusive and all encompassing. In our Lenten reflections we are to search for those things in our lives that are the other "gods." To what other gods do we bow down and worship? Do we declare God's name with our lips but in our hearts and minds forget what God has done for us and what God demands?

The law also shapes our relationships with our neighbors whom we are to love "as ourselves." Lent is a time to reflect upon and repent of those ways that we have ignored and shown contempt for those whom God has created and called us to love.

Psalm 19

Many of us have grown up in Christian communities that mistakenly contrast God's loving grace of the New Testament with the punishing law of the Old Testament. We fail to appreciate, as this psalm explores, that the law is as sweet as honey and is the way that God seeks to bring us into right relationship. This psalm will harmonize with the first reading, the giving of the law, as the community reflects on its covenantal relationship with God.

It might be helpful to lift up the multitude of ways that the psalmist has found to describe the law, the commandments, and the ordinances of God. They are: perfect, sure, right, clear, pure, true. And to what does the psalmist compare them—only those things that are most prized—gold and honey.

The community might also look at the effect that the law has on our lives. The law revives the soul, makes us wise, rejoices the heart, and enlightens the eye: what a joyous way to invite us into reflecting on the way that we are to live out the commandments.

1 Corinthians 1:18-25

While the first two lessons have focused on the laws that shape our covenantal relationship with God, the epistle and Gospel lessons focus more on the signs that point to our relationship with God. In the Gospel reading the people will ask Jesus, "What sign can you show us?" for doing what he is doing. In this reading from Paul's letter, Paul explores the baffling sign that we have been given—the cross of Christ, the death of God.

In contrast to the wonderful and joyous images in Psalm 19, Paul's letter warns us that our message will seem foolish, a stumbling block, and weak. Where, we might ask, is the good news and hope? It is, Paul reminds us, in the understanding that God's foolishness is far wiser than the wisdom of the world, and God's weakness far stronger than anything the world considers as strength and power.

Where do we look for God in our lives? How do we come to know God? We prefer to find God in the joys and successes of our lives, when we get the job we have been hoping for, or we get into the school to which we have applied. We look for God in the beauty of a mountain peak or the glorious colors of fall. Do we, however, look for or see God when a flood has ravished a community, or when we have gotten the "pink slip" telling us that we are losing our jobs? For that is what we are called to do. How foolish we are, Paul reminds us, to preach that it is the cross, that cruel instrument of death, which is, in fact, the gate to new life. Yet it is the sign of God's total love for us.

The cross, therefore, is an important theme in this reading, which also connects with the Gospel reading.

John 2:13-22

The Gospel reading continues with the theme of turning the wisdom and strength of the world on its head. In the Gospel of John, Jesus overturns the tables and drives out the moneychangers, not at the end of his ministry, as in the Synoptic Gospel accounts, but at the very start. Jesus begins his public ministry, not by preaching a comforting message of love and forgiveness, or by healing those long-suffering souls who come to follow him. Rather, he begins by clearing out all those things that keep us from God. During Lent this is a wonderful opportunity for us to overturn the tables in our lives. What practices or attitudes have we adopted that draw us away from God?

A second important theme in this lesson is the sign of the cross. How will people know who Jesus is? It is not that he will be a powerful leader in the eyes of the world. Rather, they will know him because he is so dedicated to fulfilling the mission of God that it will lead to his death on the cross. But that will not be the end. Here, at the opening of his ministry, Jesus gives us a glimpse of the end of the story. What will look like failure will end in unimaginable good news.

Where are those places in our lives that seem like failure or dead ends? How is God working to bring new life?

Year C

Isaiah 55:1-9

As in Year A, thirst is a significant theme in this reading from Isaiah. It brings us the good news that God knows our thirst and will satisfy that thirst abundantly and freely. But God also knows that we often thirst for the wrong things. Why, God asks, do we seek after those things that will not satisfy?

God seeks a relationship with us. But we wander away and squander the gift of love that has been given so freely. Isaiah reminds us that God is always seeking for us to return and awaits us with forgiveness and mercy.

This is an opportunity for us to identify those ways in our lives that we misspend our spiritual capital. How are we spending our "money" on that which ultimately will not satisfy?

Psalm 63:1-8

As I noted at the opening of this chapter, it is rare for us in North America to experience true thirst. Even if we are not carrying our own water, we are never far from a water fountain or soda machine. It is, therefore, difficult for us to imagine the extreme thirst that the psalmist alludes to in describing his intense longing for God. For some reason the psalmist perceives that God is missing from his life. And although he is searching, he trusts that he ultimately will find God.

Perhaps this is a time for those who have given up something for Lent to reflect on how much they miss that item, whether it is something to eat or drink or perhaps something to do. What has happened since that has been removed from your life? Do you miss it? Does its absence remind you that you are walking the way of the cross?

1 Corinthians 10:1-13

During Lent there is a temptation to focus on our individual spiritual journey. While this is certainly an important part of our faith life, this passage from Paul's letter to the new church members in Corinth serves as a reminder that the entire church is also on a Lenten journey. We, as the church, must not become complacent and think that we can do whatever we please because we have God's love and favor.

Paul lifts up the example of the experience of the people of Israel in the wilderness. In spite of all that God had done for them, they turned away from God and in turn were "struck down." This, he argues, should serve as an example to us lest we too turn away.

If you have people who are preparing for baptism at Easter, this passage gives you the opportunity to explore what baptism is. It is not, Paul reminds us, an inoculation against bad things happening. Nor can we, after our baptism, rest on our laurels. We will be tempted by any number of sins and vices. We have to learn how to stay on the right path.

Paul also reminds us that God may test us as the children of Israel were tested. In testing us, God will be with us and will not test us beyond our strength. I am reminded of an observation of Mother Theresa, "I know that God will not give me more than I can handle. I just wish he didn't trust me so much."

Luke 13:1-9

When we encounter the tragedies of others, a small voice deep inside us quietly whispers, "*thank goodness that didn't happened to me!*" We also search for reasons that it did happen to the other person. Was that person in the wrong place at the wrong time? Did that person do something wrong? Hidden in those questions is an important question—are there things that I should or should not be doing that will prevent that tragedy from striking the ones I love or me?

Those following Jesus were no different. When reflecting on the execution of several Galileans, they wondered whether those persons had died because they had done something wrong. Unfortunately, the Jesus we encounter in this moment is not the pastoral, gentle Jesus we prefer. Instead of assuring his followers that they will be all right and that a similar fate does not await them, he challenges their way of thinking.

The people killed by Pilate, Jesus declares, were not greater sinners than they. Likewise, those killed in an apparent construction accident were also sinners. And we—Jesus seems to be saying—we are all sinners. If his followers do not repent, he says, they may meet a similar fate.

Where, we might ask, is the good news in this terrifying picture? It comes in the parable of the fig tree. Yes, God demands our very best. We, as individuals and as church, are to live lives that bear the fruit of love and compassion. If those lives are barren, the tree of life may be removed from the garden. But this is a story of second chances. Thanks be to God we have been given a patient and forgiving gardener in the person of Jesus. He is willing to tend us and work with us over and over again until we blossom and bear the fruit of righteousness.

Lent is an opportunity to examine our lives. We are called by Jesus to repent of our sins and turn to him. Are our lives fruitful, or is our faith life one of bare branches?

WORSHIP AND PREACHING THEMES

- **Thirst** is a recurring theme through many of the lessons. They contrast our strong thirst for God—which should be encouraged—with those who thirst in physical need and want, as well as our thirsts for power, fortune, and fame.
- **Water** is, therefore, another theme. Our need and thirst for water, without which we will perish, is an analogy for our need and thirst for God. Without God, we will surely perish. We see God's overflowing, abundant gift of water that pours forth from an unlikely

place—solid rock. We are reminded that Jesus is the living water that brings us eternal life.

- The ways that we **test, quarrel with,** and **complain to** God are found in a number of the readings. People question whether or not God is there, in spite of all that God has done for them. People ask Jesus if others are greater sinners than they are. We also see Jesus clearing the temple of those whose actions tested God's presence in the temple.
- Another crucial theme is **feasting** and God's generous offer of abundant food. God is there to meet our needs.

CREATING THE ENVIRONMENT

- Water occurs in a number of readings. If your worship space and budget permit, you might purchase a fountain. There are some available that look as though the water is pouring forth from a rock. Or, you might place a large, clear glass bowl filled with water at the center of your worship space.
- The water poured out of a rock. You may put several large rocks in front of the congregation.
- In Year B we read that Jesus cleansed the temple. If your worship space includes a narthex or entry hall, you might remove everything that is normally in that space.
- When you read the passage of the fig tree bearing fruit, you may have either trees in full leaf, or you may have trees with bare branches in the worship space.

SHAPING THE WORSHIP SERVICE

Music
- "I've Got Peace Like a River," African American Spiritual

- "Out of the Depths, O God, We Call to You," by Ruth Duck
- "Come, All of You," Laotian Hymn, trans. by Cher Lue Vang
- "Fill My Cup, Lord," by Richard Blanchard
- "O Love, How Deep," 15th cent. Latin, trans. By Benjamin Webb
- "The Welcome Table," African American Spiritual
- "Surely It Is God Who Saves Me," Isa 12:2-6, paraphrased by Carl P. Daw Jr.
- "As the Deer," by Martin J. Nystrom

Opening the Service

Call to Worship (based on Psalm 95)

O come, let us sing to the Lord:
Let us make a joyful noise to the rock of our salvation!
Let us come into God's presence with thanksgiving;
Let us make a joyful noise to God with songs of praise!
O come, let us worship and bow down,
Let us kneel before the Lord, our Maker!

Opening Procession

While the community sings "Come, All of You," a Laotian hymn, you may have people walk to the front of the worship space carrying bowls or pitchers of water, milk, and grape juice, and large loaves of bread showing us signs of God's abundant grace.

Opening Prayer

Great and loving God,
        you fill our lives full to overflowing with your grace.
We come as weary travelers in a barren land,
        parched, longing for your life-giving word,
Open our hearts and minds to hear that word spoken anew.
Let it pour over us as the water that renews and revives.

All this we ask in the name of him who is living water,
Jesus the Christ. **Amen.**

Service of the Word

*The Gospel reading in Year A (John 4:5-42), the encounter between
Jesus and the woman of Samaria, would work well as a dramatic reading. With one person as narrator, one as the woman, and one as Jesus,
the chorus could then read the parts of the disciples and the people of
Samaria.*

Confession and Pardon

Prayer of Confession

Gracious and most merciful God,
>we come before you
>>admitting that we are your bickering,
>>complaining children.
You have showered us with love and affection.
You have filled our lives with gifts of
>graciousness and new life,
>>but we, in our selfishness and greed,
>>turn away from you.
We quarrel with you and test you.
We want more. We do not trust.
Remove our hardened hearts of stone,
>and give us hearts to love you with
>thankfulness and praise.
Let the words of our mouths and
>the meditations of our hearts
>be acceptable to you,
O Lord, our rock and our redeemer. Amen.

Words of Assurance and Pardon

God is our rock from which flows
>the flood of forgiveness.

Through God's grace our hearts of stone
become hearts of flesh.
May God have mercy on us
and bring us to new life in Christ Jesus.

Closing the Service

If you have a closing processional out of the worship space, you may have people carry out the bowls of water that were carried into the service. As they leave, they might dip branches into the water and sprinkle the congregation with water, reminding them of their baptism and God's abundant living water that fills their lives.

FOURTH SUNDAY IN LENT

WHICH PATH?

During our Lenten journey we reflect upon the path that is our life, both as individuals and as a community. It is a path that we all know is filled with unexpected twists and turns, joyous ups and painful downs. Several of the lessons today explore those moments when we take the wrong path; when we head off to do it "our way." Unfortunately, all too often, our way leads us away from God and toward the way of suffering and death.

Lent is an opportunity to reflect upon the paths we have chosen. Are we on the right path? Are we on the way to the one who is "the way, the truth, and the light?" And, if we find that we have wandered off in the wrong direction—if we have taken the wrong path—Lent gives us the opportunity to confess our misdirection, reflect on God's grace and mercy, and make a course correction. We can return to the God who is waiting for us. No, more than that, Luke reminds us that we have a God who, in fact, is running out to meet us even when we are far off.

Our roads are filled with signs that give us direction and guide us on the right path. We search for street signs or highway markers.

Stop signs and one-way markers keep traffic in an orderly flow and, on the whole, prevent accidents. The Scriptures provide us with the same signs and markers. They help us know what path to follow.

SITTING WITH THE TEXT

Year A

1 Samuel 16:1-13

We take great comfort in the story of the anointing of the young shepherd boy, David, by the great prophet, Samuel. The story reminds us that God can choose the lowliest, the almost forgotten, and use them to do great things. This story gives us hope that God will see in each of us something worthy, for God declares that God does not see as human beings see.

As we read this story, however, we must not forget that this is a story of risk, mistrust, and shock. Samuel is taking a risk to venture out looking for Saul's replacement. Saul had wandered off on the wrong path and was taking the people with him. When sent by God on this mission, Samuel does not want to go. He knows what will await him if Saul discovers what he is doing. Saul could have him killed.

Samuel is uncertain and does not trust God. As he looks at all of the handsome and strong sons of Jesse, he sees many young men who could be potential leaders. But as he looks at each one, God admonishes Samuel, telling him to wait. Samuel is not to pick the leader. That is God's doing.

This is a shocking story. Why would God choose the youngest and smallest of all of Jesse's sons? Why does God choose the weak to confront the powerful? We know that David will eventually confront and conquer Goliath. We know that David will unify the kingdoms. We know that David, for all his flaws, will become the great king. But, at this moment of his anointing, that is all in the future and David seems an unlikely choice. Given the political situation with Saul, why does God pick a young boy?

In the end, this is, then, a story of David—the new leader who comes out of Bethlehem, the one who will subvert and overthrow those in power. But it is also a story of Samuel's obedience to God, anointing the man of God's choosing.

Where do you see God doing surprising, shocking things? Is God asking you to take a great risk? Does God see greater potential in you than you do in yourself? Does your faith community feel like a "David" in a world of Goliaths?

Psalm 23

Having just read the story of the choosing and anointing of the new "shepherd" of Israel, the shepherd boy David, the accompanying psalm reminds us that no human shepherd can ever supplant our divine shepherd. Only God can lead us through the darkest moments of our lives to places of comfort and refreshment. At the end of the first reading we do well to remember that David will become a great leader, not through his own power and strength, but because "the spirit of the Lord came mightily upon" him.

During our Lenten journey we are given these words of love and encouragement. The psalm paints a beautiful image of God's presence in our lives—a green place beside clear, refreshing water.

Ephesians 5:8-14

A recurring theme in the Lenten lessons addresses our human tendency to take our life in God for granted and to ignore the ethical implications of the new life that we have been given through the death and resurrection of Jesus. In this portion of the letter to the Ephesians, Paul reminds them of this new life—that once they were dark (notice that he tells them that they "were darkness" not *in* darkness), and now they are light.

But what does it mean to live as the light of God? In the Gospel lesson we will hear again of the contrast between light and dark, and we will hear Jesus declare that he is the "light of the world." Paul reminds us that we too are to live a life that can be seen in the daylight. Whatever we do we should not mind people watching us. How would you live if you were in a reality program and someone was recording your every move?

If people in your community are preparing for baptism, this text is an important opportunity to explore the difference that baptism makes—the move from darkness to light. We become, through baptism, the light of the world that is not to be hidden under a basket.

John 9:1-41

With the themes of darkness, light, and seeing as God sees versus human blindness, we turn to the story of Jesus healing a blind man. This is a wonderfully long and complex drama, and John invites us into reflection on a number of important questions. It is critical, therefore, not to focus solely on this miraculous healing at the expense of the story in which this healing occurs, for this is a story that will help us in our Lenten reflections. How are we blind to our sins and to God's presence in our lives?

This is a multiple-act play. It begins with an exchange between Jesus and his disciples, who have spotted a blind beggar seated by the side of the road. The disciples are not thinking about healing the man; rather, they view him as an opportunity to discuss sin. Was this man's blindness caused by his sin or by the sins of his parents? We do well to keep this question before us for, although Jesus disabuses the disciples of this understanding, in the end it is our sin of arrogance that causes us to be blind to God's healing touch in our lives.

We should note that the man does not approach Jesus and ask for healing; rather, Jesus prepares an anointing mud of dirt and saliva that he spreads on the man's eyes. Jesus does not ask the man if he might heal him. Jesus' only exchange with the man is to tell him to go and wash. Jesus seems to be too busy teaching the disciples; the man is there so that Jesus can demonstrate that he is the light of the world who brings grace and healing.

Until the exchange between this unnamed man and Jesus at the close of the drama, Jesus and the disciples disappear. Instead, we turn our attention to the confusion and accusations caused by this amazing healing. How can this be? Who has done this? Who would dare heal on the Sabbath? The social order has been upset and those in charge question not only the man but also his parents so that they might know whom to properly accuse.

This is a story about a healing. But it is also a story about how we come to know God. As God acted in the story of David, it is Jesus who takes the initiative. We know God; we are chosen by God because God has sought us out. God has acted first. But miraculous signs are not enough. The man could see, but that did not necessarily make him a follower of Jesus. After his gift of sight he was accused and persecuted. It was only when he encountered Jesus that he came to truly see.

Year B

Numbers 21:4-9

The Israelites thought God had taken them off on the wrong path. As they wandered in the wilderness, they began to wonder if they were, in fact, being led not to a land of promise but to their death in the middle of nowhere. Whining, complaining, and quarreling seem to have been a common refrain. This time, however, God's reaction is troubling. The complaints of the Israelites provoke God to make a seemingly petulant response. Their camp is suddenly filled with poisonous snakes, sent by God, that proceed to bite these complaining people on the ankle.

Which is more troubling for modern readers, the punishment or the cure? Although God punishes the ill-tempered flock, God also provides a way out, a penitential response when they show remorse. We, who live in an age of medicines, vaccines, and surgery, have a difficult time deciding what to make of the directions to look at a bronze serpent that is "lifted up," on a pole. Nevertheless, it seems to be just what was needed.

This text is chosen for the image of the bronze sculpture being lifted up. In today's Gospel reading from John, Jesus reminds

Nicodemus that he is like that serpent, sent to save those who look upon him. In the end we will want to focus more on God's mercy and the grace God provides to those in need. We look upon the cross not as an instrument of torture and death but one that gives new life.

Psalm 107:1-3, 17-22

Who are these people that are being called from east and west, north and south? The Psalms are filled with intriguing mysteries. The psalmist may be referring to the Israelites. They were made sick by their sinful ways. And, as we read in the other Old Testament passage for today, they did loathe their "miserable food." But we can also identify with those who cry out to God in the moment of trouble.

This is a psalm that reminds us of God's patience and love. The psalmist declares that, in spite of the troubles that afflict us, God's "steadfast love endures forever." This might be a wonderful refrain to weave throughout the service. We cannot hear this message too often. You will not have difficulty finding people in the congregation who will eagerly tell the story of how they have experienced God's steadfast love.

Ephesians 2:1-10

In every journey there is a moment when you stop your forward progress and look back to see where you have been and how far you have come. Paul is encouraging those on the journey of faith to stop and reflect upon where they are in their journey. They once were dead; now they are alive. They once were captive to the sins of the world; now they have been saved. But Paul wants them—wants us—to remember that this is not of our own doing. We cannot save ourselves. We can never work hard enough to earn the great gifts that we have been given, because they are just that, *gifts* from God.

The letter is helpful for setting before us the paths that are available to us, the path of grace and faith or the path of trespass and sin. Lent is a time to reflect on the choices that we have made and that we need to make every day.

John 3:14-21

Today's Gospel reading is taken from the exchange between Jesus and Nicodemus. The fuller text of that conversation is the reading for the Second Sunday in Lent, Year A.

Jesus is setting God's plan before the inquisitive Nicodemus. God, Jesus reminds the teacher of the law, loves the world so much that God will do whatever it takes to save the wayward world—even to the point of death. From the very opening of the exchange, Jesus points to the event that will take place at Calvary. He, like the bronze serpent, will be lifted up so that all who see him will find healing and wholeness (see v. 14).

It is important that we recognize that this is God's action. God has taken the initiative. God sent the Son. God provides the light that will lead us on the right path.

Year C

The Scriptures are filled with moments of forgiveness and reconciliation. The readings for this year focus on those moments of new life.

Joshua 5:9-12

The reading from Joshua records an important moment in the life of the people of Israel. It is the moment when they leave their life of wandering in the wilderness and settle in the land that God had promised them. But in the midst of recounting this key moment, the author is told by God to report to the people that God has "rolled away . . . the disgrace of Egypt." While we are not told what that particular disgrace is, it is, nevertheless, a moment of forgiveness and new life.

You might reflect on a time in your life when you had that intense feeling of being forgiven by God or by someone for something that you had done.

Psalm 32

Most of us have experienced those terrible moments when we know that we have done something wrong, but we cannot bring ourselves to confess that wrong and ask for forgiveness. We do not know the nature of the psalmist's transgression, but we do know that it was something that the writer hid and would not publicly acknowledge. While the psalm records this painful moment, it is not the end of the story. This is not a psalm about sin as much as it is about the acknowledgment of that sin and God's forgiving nature. It is about confession and about absolution, about guilt and about pardon.

2 Corinthians 5:16-21

In this reading, we hear of Paul's understanding of forgiveness and reconciliation. In Christ we have been forgiven; our disgrace, like the Israelites, has been rolled away. In the light of the resurrection, everything has changed; everything has been made new. God does not look at us the same way, we do not look on Christ the same way, and we are challenged to look on one another in a new way.

When we live as new creatures who have experienced the release from sin, we are not to rest on our laurels. Rather, we are sent into the world to "go and do likewise." We are to be ministers of reconciliation. We are to let all people know that Christ came that they might have life and have it abundantly. We are to show the world what it means to live as the body of Christ. They will know us by our love.

Luke 15:1-3; 11b-32

Who is the *star* of this show? Is it the wayward son who breaks his father's heart? Is it the faithful but frigid son who seems to despise both brother and father? Or is it the foolish father who gives half of his fortune to a son he doubtless knows will squander the money?

The story of a man and his two sons is probably one of the top five best known Bible stories. Every day, people refer to someone as a "prodigal son" without knowing the story (or what *prodigal* means—recklessly extravagant, not returning.) It is important, therefore, to seek to enter into this story with fresh eyes and ears, as if for the first time. We do that by first lifting up the reason that Jesus told the story.

Jesus was prodigal with his love and friendship. He recklessly ate and communed with the outcasts and pariahs of the village. He showed us that we are the children of a God who accepts everyone, saints and sinners alike. And so he told us this rich story of "our Father," a father who is equally prodigal with his love and forgiveness.

We might compare and contrast the two paths taken by two very different brothers. The older brother stays home, works, and feels overburdened and neglected. Is this the right path? The younger brother leaves home and seems to have chosen the wrong path. He wastes his inheritance and clearly ends up at the bottom of the ash heap. He realizes that he is on the path that leads to destruction and death. Ultimately, his is a path of confession and *metanoia*—turning, repentance. The younger son finally "came to himself." Is this the right path?

Which path leads to the loving embrace of the father? Which path leads to the banquet that prefigures the heavenly banquet that God has prepared for all who turn to God? Are we ready to turn and return to the one who is always more ready to forgive than we are to confess? Jesus has given us an amazing portrait of a father who was always scanning the horizon for his exasperating but still beloved son. This is a father who never gave up hope. This is a father who is, in the words of Joshua, ready to "roll away . . . the disgrace" even before his son utters a word of confession. The son is still out on the road when the father directs his servants to begin preparing the feast.

Crucial to all of this, however, is the son's willingness to admit that he was on the wrong path and his willingness to humble himself before his father. Forgiveness and reconciliation lie at the end of our Lenten journey, but we must be willing to turn and walk that path.

WORSHIP AND PREACHING THEMES

- The themes of **healing** and **reconciliation** run through a number of the texts for this Fourth Sunday in Lent. The man who was born blind received his sight. Those who were attacked by snakes in the wilderness are healed when they look upon the bronzed serpent. The young man who found himself lost and hopeless finds that new life is possible in the love of his father.
- Likewise, the themes of **forgiveness** and **acceptance** accompany the theme of healing. All too often we find that God is more willing to forgive and accept us than we are to forgive ourselves. Lent is an opportunity to celebrate God's love and also to forgive ourselves. The people of Israel are forgiven. The young son is forgiven. We are forgiven.
- God's **grace** is an important theme this week. All too often, we slip into thinking that we need to earn God's forgiveness. We think that we need to be *good* children so that God will love us. Whether it is in the story of the man born blind or the young son, God makes the first move. They are healed and forgiven before they have a chance to do anything. It truly is amazing grace.
- **Light** serves as a metaphor for insight and recognition. The man born blind receives his sight, but his family and community remain blind to the light of God shining in their midst. The young man sees the light of love and possible new life when he is in the darkest moment of his life. How often do we ignore the light that is there to light our way?

CREATING THE ENVIRONMENT

Throughout the Lenten journey, the goal has been to create a fairly stark worship environment—forgoing the use of flowers or anything that detracts from the sharpness of the call to repentance on the way of the cross. But the Fourth Sunday in Lent offers relief. The lessons talk about healing, forgiveness, and reconciliation.

In the Roman Catholic Church, the Fourth Sunday in Lent is known as *Laetare* Sunday—a name taken from the opening of the service, "*Laetare Jerusalem*"—"O be joyful Jerusalem." It became a time for a respite during the Lenten journey. Flowers are allowed and, if a congregation is wealthy enough, it will have a separate set of vestments. Rather than the purple of Lent, the clergy will wear rose-colored vestments. (Unfortunately, they often look more like Pepto-Bismol pink.) This Sunday corresponds with the third Sunday in the Advent journey, *Gaudete* Sunday, (*Gaudete* means rejoice) when a pink or rose candle on the Advent wreath is lighted and the rose-colored vestments would also be worn.

I suspect that you will not want to rush out and invest in a set of rose-colored vestments, but you may think about a way to mark this Sunday's themes of love, grace, forgiveness, and reconciliation.

It could be a time to make use of rose-colored drapes or pink flowers. For many, this will be a time when spring flowers are appearing. You might place vases of budding branches on the altar—signs that life is returning.

Light is another important theme of some of the lessons this week. You might think of filling the worship space with candles to remind us that we have come together to worship the "light of the world."

SHAPING THE WORSHIP SERVICE

Music

- "Amazing Grace! How Sweet the Sound," by John Newton
- "The Lord's My Shepherd, I'll Not Want," Scottish Psalter
- "The King of Love My Shepherd Is," by Henry W. Baker
- "I Want to Walk as a Child of the Light," by Kathleen Thomerson

- "Gather Us In," by Marty Haugen
- "Be Still for the Presence of the Lord," by David Evans
- "Like the Murmur of the Dove's Song," by Carl P. Daw
- "Peace for the Children," by Doreen Lankshear-Smith
- "Lay Your Hands," by Carey Landry and Carol Jean Kinghorn

Opening the Service

Call to Worship

From near and far you have called us,
　　you have sought us out.
The Lord is our Shepherd.
You have brought us out of darkness into light.
With you we are able to walk through
　　the valley of the shadow of death.
Our Lord is the light of the world.
We who were dead have been brought to life.
We who were lost have been found.

Alternative Opening

With the recurring theme of being lost and being found, you might play with this idea: place people, unobtrusively, around the edges of your worship space, perhaps some members of a choir or music group that play and sing at the front of the worship space. Another member of the group, calling their names as if looking for them, walks into the worship space and toward the front. Standing at the front, this person continues calling their names as the congregation begins to sing "Amazing Grace." The "lost" then begin to appear from around the room and make their way toward the front while they, with the congregation, continue to sing—the lost have been found.

Opening Prayer

Holy and gracious God,
you who have offered us abundant, new life;

be with us as we answer the call of your son Jesus
to walk in his light.
May we, who sit in the darkness of sin and selfishness,
awaken to your ever present love.
This we ask in the name of Jesus
through the power of the Holy Spirit.
Amen.

Service of the Word

The Gospel readings for years A (John 9:1-41) and C (Luke 15:1-3; 11b-32) easily lend themselves to dramatic readings. They have characters, drama, and movement. They are opportunities to involve a number of people in the telling of the story and, in doing so, make these stories live. No rewriting needs to be done except turning the narrative into a script.

Confession and Pardon

Litany of Confession

It is an uncomfortable moment when,
like the prodigal son,
we realize that we have traveled down the wrong path.
We feel afraid and adrift.
Yet in that moment of anxiety and panic,
we are to remember that we are not alone.
In the valley of the shadow of death
we are to fear no evil, for our God is with us always.
Let us therefore confess our sins to
our loving and forgiving God.
Almighty and all loving God.
We come before you as your disobedient children.
We have gone our own way.
We have disregarded your guidance and direction.
We have ignored our sisters and brothers in need.
We are lost and wayward.
Have mercy and forgive us.

Help us see that you are waiting for us to return.
Help us turn and take the first step.
This we ask in the name of Jesus, Emmanuel,
God with us.

Words of Assurance and Pardon

We proclaim God is with us.
God is with us pardoning, forgiving,
> welcoming us into the loving arms of our creator
> parent.
Even while we were yet far off, God searched for us,
> longing for our return.
And when we acknowledge our sin and return,
> it is with celebration and rejoicing
> that we are welcomed back into the community.
Thanks be to God who gives us the victory of new life.
Amen.

Prayers

In preparation for the prayers, the worship team will need to review current news. Those headlines will appear in the prayers. For this book, I went to the newspaper and drew on those things that were making headlines as I wrote—you will prepare your own.

The readers are to announce the headlines while using a questioning and uncertain tone, as though they are not sure what to do in the face of this pain and suffering. At the close of the prayers, their tone should shift to confidence and reassurance.

Reader One: An explosion killed six American soldiers yesterday!

All Readers: May God have mercy.

Reader Two: The bodies of four young girls were found dead in their own home. They had been dead for months.

Reader Three: Mercy!

Reader Two: The police think that their mother killed them.

All Readers: God have mercy.

Reader Four:	And a father threw his four children from a bridge.
All Readers:	Holy God, we turn to you.
Reader Three:	In Kenya people continue to riot and kill, angered by the election returns.
All Readers:	Holy God, hear our cries.
Reader Three:	We pray for those who are ill and alone.
Reader Four:	We pray for those who are lost and abandoned.
Reader One:	We pray for the oppressed and those in prison.
Reader Two:	And we know that we pray to the one who knows our prayers even before we utter them.
Reader Four:	We know that you love us and will never leave us.
Reader Three:	For you are our God and we are your children. Comfort and support us.
All Readers:	And grant us peace, now and always. Amen.

Closing the Service

Go into the world walking the path of God.
Peace be with us.
Go into the world walking in the way of the cross.
Peace be with us.
Go into the world filled with the Spirit.
Peace be with us.

CHAPTER SEVEN

FIFTH SUNDAY IN LENT

LIKE THOSE WHO DREAM

As we arrive at the Fifth Sunday in Lent, we know that our journey is almost at an end. Like children on a driving trip, we are tempted to ask, "Are we there yet?" The answer is yes and no. No, we have almost two weeks left until our church is filled with lilies, the sweet scent of resurrection. Therefore, as Paul reminds us, we live in the time of the already and the not yet.

But on this Sunday, the week before Palm Sunday, we are given glimpses and foreshadowing of the story that will shortly unfold before us, that of the passion, death, and resurrection of Jesus. The texts this day speak of death and new life made possible by our God. The words of God call us to expect the unexpected, to dream of the impossible. As the psalmist reminds us, when we remember what God has done for us in the past and think ahead to what God has yet to do, we are like those who dream.

Unfortunately, we live in a world that makes it hard to be dreamers. Dreams, visions, and hopes for new life are quickly dismissed as impossible, foolish, and unrealistic. Yet we know we have experienced those moments of the impossible when we, like Ezekiel, have seen dry bones flourish or the desert bloom. Those glimpses stun and startle us, but we also know that they do not mean the journey is over. They come as gifts that strengthen us for the journey that continues until we finally gather together at the heavenly banquet that has been spread for us by our loving God. This week we will celebrate with Mary, Martha, Peter, and Paul as they proclaim that death is not the end, and we will focus on glimpses of glory and dreams of new life.

SITTING WITH THE TEXT

Year A

Ezekiel 37:1-3 (4-10) 11-14

Do you think that Ezekiel knows what he is seeing when he is taken to that valley of dry bones? We certainly don't always understand the visions that God places before us.

For Ezekiel the meaning quickly becomes clear. God wants him to see that new life is possible for the people of Israel who continue in exile. It is not the end; the time is coming when, through the words of the prophet and the power of God, those dry bones will be covered with flesh and filled with life-giving breath. These words are not eschatological but political. They refer to a real people at a real time in a real place. And as such, they can also inspire us to know that when we answer God's call and work with God, new life is possible for people who are oppressed and living lives that seem dead.

But we also read this lesson on the Fifth Sunday in Lent because it introduces important themes for us as we prepare to walk the way of the cross. It gives us a word of hope and encouragement. Through the power of God, what seem like death and failure are, in fact, not the end. We will ask this same question as we approach the tomb in the garden, "Can these bones live?" And when we do, we will already know the answer—Indeed!

Can you think of a moment when you were given a glimpse of something that had seemed dead come to life?

Psalm 130

Again we hear the theme of hope in the midst of despair. This is a psalm about anguish—about someone who has come to the very bottom of life's journey. We might think of this as the cry of the dry bones in the field. It is a prayer of anguish, but not one of hopelessness.

We do not know the circumstances of this person. We do not know if it is an individual or a collective cry. In the opening of the psalm, it is the cry of one; by the end, the psalmist urges Israel—the whole nation—to hope in the God who will forgive and redeem. The psalmist reminds the nation and reminds us that our lives are in the hands of a loving, forgiving, and most important, loyal God. Ours is a God we can trust.

Romans 8:6-11

Paul presents his readers with an important distinction, the realm of the flesh and the realm of the spirit. As we explore what it means to live in the spirit, which Paul reminds us leads to life and peace, we must be careful not to set up a destructive dualism. Paul does not mean to say that our flesh, our bodies are bad. Rather, he wants us to understand the difference between following our own desires and following God's will. Do we want to do it our way, or do we want to do it God's way?

The important focus in the reading for us, as we move into the week of the passion, is Paul's strong message that the death and resurrection of Jesus, accomplished through the Spirit of God, is at the center of our faith. The breath of God that moved over the waters at creation, that filled those dry bones, "raised Christ from the dead," and that will give us new life.

John 11:1-45

This intense, multilayered story provides a number of directions for those planning worship and preparing to preach from this text.

It is difficult not to focus in on the miracle of the resuscitation of Lazarus. Like those standing at the mouth of the tomb, we listen in amazement as we are told that Lazarus—three days dead, sealed in the tomb—walks. How can this be? Dead people do not get up and walk about. It must seem like a dream. But there in front of them stands the man who made the impossible possible, the dead—alive.

The conversation between Jesus and Martha also turns our attention to the proclamation that Jesus is "the resurrection and the life." The focus here is not so much on Jesus as it is on what happens to us after we die.

However, given the context in which we are hearing this story told anew—as we prepare to walk the way of the cross—we will want to make the connections between this story and the story of Jesus' death and resurrection. Lazarus is not the first person that Jesus has resuscitated (see Luke 7:14-15; 8:52-55), but it is his resuscitation that captures the attention of the authorities and, according to John, will play an important part in leading to the crucifixion of Jesus. Throughout this amazing story are allusions to the events that are about to unfold. This sign is not about Lazarus; it is about Jesus. Jesus acts so that people will turn their attention to the Son of God. We hear that Lazarus has been in the tomb for three days—the time necessary for the soul to leave the body. Jesus will be in the tomb for three days. Jesus' heart is heavy—not only for Mary and Martha, not only for the death of his friend but also for what lies ahead of him. It is important, therefore, to focus on the connections between this story and the passion narrative. This helps us begin to look for life in the midst of death.

Have you had a "Lazarus moment"? Have there been times in your life, in the life of your congregation when you discovered that you had been given another chance?

Year B

Jeremiah 31:31-34

Throughout the Lenten journey we have been reflecting on our relationships with God and our relationships with one another. Jeremiah reminds us that, in the end, it is God who will repair and renew those relationships; we cannot do it on our own.

Clearly, those who had been carried into exile and captivity felt that they had betrayed God and therefore had been abandoned by God. They also lived in the fear that their relationship, the covenant God had made with them, was forever shattered. Not so, declares God through the prophet Jeremiah. This wild character, who had once pronounced only judgment, now comes with words of comfort. God will forgive and will wipe away all the obstacles between them.

Psalm 51:1-12

It was with this psalm that we began the observance of Lent on Ash Wednesday. Now, as our journey of reflection and repentance comes to the climax of Holy Week, we once again hear the cry for forgiveness.

Reflecting on those who may be preparing for baptism, we might pay close attention to the words of purification that are woven through the psalm: blot out, wash me, cleanse me, purge me, create a clean heart, a new spirit, restore. Through the death and resurrection of Christ we have become new creations. You might reflect upon what that means in your life today. How does it feel being a new creation? How would you explain that to someone preparing for baptism?

Hebrews 5:5-10

After the resurrection, the followers of the man who died and was raised sought to understand who he was and what all of this meant. For the writer of the letter to the Hebrews, the categories and frame of reference that were most helpful for the people to whom the author was writing were those of the Jewish world. To understand this man who was obedient even unto death, the author turned to an ancient hero—the high priest Melchizedek. Jesus, like the high priest of old, offered a sacrifice, but he was the sacrifice. It will not be easy for most people today to appreciate the complexity of the argument.

John 12:20-33

The theme of suffering and death that was introduced in the letter to the Hebrews continues in John's Gospel. Crowds were gathering in Jerusalem for the celebration of the Passover. In the city that teemed with excitement, Jesus was making big news. After his spectacular entry into the city, a group of people from Greece approached Jesus' disciples requesting an audience with this celebrity. Whether or not they ever met Jesus is not clear from the text. Is Jesus speaking to the Greeks or is he speaking to Philip and Andrew?

What is interesting is the juxtaposition of the question with the answer. What will we *see* if we see Jesus? Jesus tells us that we will see someone who must die.

Throughout John's Gospel, Jesus repeatedly tells people that things cannot happen because his "hour has not yet come" (John 2:4; 7:30; 8:20). But now the hour has finally come. It is the hour for Jesus to glorify God and to be glorified, in turn, by God. Using the image of a wheat grain, Jesus declares that his death is necessary in order to bear the fruit of new life. Jesus helps us understand a truth that is woven through the scriptures—God's ways are not our ways. God does not see as humans see. We may think that the grain of wheat put in the ground is dead; but it is the beginning. Only after planting will the grain grow and produce fruit.

Jesus presents us with a vision, an understanding to hold on to as we enter into the story of that moment that feels like failure, the passion and death of the teacher. We are to realize, he declares, that only through his death will we have life.

Year C

Isaiah 43:16-21

With this reading from Isaiah we return to contemplation on the theme of wilderness. On Ash Wednesday and the First Sunday in Lent, the opening of our Lenten journey, we reflected upon our entrance into the wilderness. But in this reading, Isaiah does not use the image of wilderness as a place of foreboding. Rather, he declares that, in the wilderness, our God has done and will continue to do amazing things. He presents us with a series of stunning images that emphasize what startling things God can do.

We must remember that Isaiah is writing to people who are still in exile. They are wondering if God has abandoned them. So, while Isaiah begins reminding the people that God brought them out of slavery in Egypt by parting the waters, he then makes a rather contradictory charge. We are to forget the former things and look only forward. Are we to forget what God has done, or are we to forget the difficulties in our lives? Either way, God will continue to surprise in the future. God will fill the desert with water. Vicious animals and giant birds will join the human choruses singing God's praises. Does this sound like any dreams that you have had?

The hymn that we are to sing as we walk to the end of our Lenten journey is: "Our God is doing new things. Our God is making a way in the wilderness. Our God is doing great things."

Psalm 126

Like Isaiah, the psalmist is speaking to those living through difficult times. They are sowing tears, they are weeping, and they toil for others. The psalmist lifts up God's heroic deeds of the past to remind them that they are not alone; they have not been abandoned. If they will but remember what God has done for them, they will once again be "like those who dream." It is a challenge to dream once more, to see visions of what God can and will do, to not give up.

This psalm was sung while people were on a religious pilgrimage. As we draw near to the end of our Lenten pilgrimage, this psalm reminds us to keep our eyes on God's future actions.

Philippians 3:4b-14

It must have been rather shocking for the friends of Paul when he returned from his trip to Damascus. Their friend, who had been ferociously seeking to discredit and destroy the followers of the crucified rabbi, Jesus, had now become one of those followers. How could this be? I suspect that many of them thought that Paul had fallen under a demonic spell. Yet here he is, writing to the new Christians in Philippi that he is neither possessed nor crazy.

Rather, his life has taken a complete turn. Everything that had mattered to him, those things that had made him important and given him status in the community, he now counts as rubbish. To follow Jesus means a complete shift in values and identity.

As we prepare to walk the way of the cross, Paul reminds us that our whole lives are to be lived in the way of the cross. We are to die to our old way of life, the way of the world. And in doing so, we will live into the power of the resurrection.

During our Lenten walk, many of us have given up certain things to eat or drink. Now Paul challenges us to think about much greater things. What must we give up and renounce? What are we to count as "rubbish?" How might we turn our lives completely around? What would you need to do in following God that might make your family and friends think that you were crazy or possessed?

John 12:1-8

John presents his telling of an important story in the life of Jesus—his anointing with oil by a woman. Who was this woman? When did it happen? John tells us that it is Mary, the friend of Jesus and sister of Martha and Lazarus, who anoints his feet shortly before his entry into Jerusalem and the events that end on the cross. Yet Mark and Matthew do not indicate that this woman is Mary. In fact, Matthew tells us that she is a woman of rather questionable reputation. Whoever she is, Mark tells us that what she does is absolutely crucial and would be remembered forever.

Mary's prophetic act signals to all who are gathered around the table that Jesus is moving toward death. The hour has finally come and Mary knows it. They are gathered for dinner. The only other time John uses this word, *deipnon* ("dinner" or "supper"), is in reference to the last supper with the disciples. For Mary this is an extravagant display of her love and affection. Think what happens if you break a bottle of perfume—you can smell it all over the house. In this way Mary tells Jesus that she knows what is going to happen and that, not only will she prepare him for this, she will be with him and not abandon him. That is our call as we move into the final events of Lent—to be faithful disciples.

WORSHIP AND PREACHING THEMES

- As we begin to move into the intense period of Holy Week, the texts chosen for this week are filled with images of **death**—the valley of dry bones, Lazarus in the tomb. While death is the end for all of us, we live in a culture that hides and ignores this reality. It is not easy for us to speak of death; and yet the church is the right place, perhaps the only place, that must be willing to help us face this reality and what it means to live and die in the Lord.

- While death is a theme woven through the texts this week, so too is the theme of **hope**. We are presented with many images that seek to awaken in us an openness to the future of God's reality. In the face of a world filled with pain and death, hope is perhaps the most difficult way to live. Only with God's help can we live into and offer hope to this broken world.

- **Cleansing** is another important theme in this week's lessons. Throughout Lent we have been seeking to wash ourselves clean. Some of us have given up things that draw our attention away from God. As people in your community are preparing for baptism, we can reflect on the ways that God makes us clean, makes us new people.

- We don't like to think about being **obedient**. We live in a culture that prizes freedom. In fact, one of the only times that we hear people talk about obedience is when it applies to dogs—dogs are sent to obedience school. Might we think about church as "obedience school"? We hear of Ezekiel's obedience to God, working with God to bring the nation of Israel back to life. We hear of Mary obediently anointing the feet of Jesus, and of Paul following obediently into his new life. But the primary image of obedience and the one after whom we all follow is Jesus, whose obedience to God has brought us all life.

CREATING THE ENVIRONMENT

The respite of the Fourth Sunday in Lent is replaced with stark preparation for Holy Week. In Year A the budding branches should be replaced with bare branches that echo the dry as dust bones that Ezekiel saw. In Year B, when Jesus speaks of the grain of wheat that must die, you might have urns filled with stalks of wheat. These are usually available at florists or hobby shops. And in Year C, as we hear the story of Mary anointing Jesus with nard—you might burn some incense so that the air is scented (although some people are bothered by strong scents). Another possibility is to have bouquets of dried lavender branches. Lavender was one of the species of nard.

SHAPING THE WORSHIP SERVICE

Music

- "Out of the Depths I Cry to You," by Martin Luther
- "Wellspring of Wisdom," by Miriam Therese Winter
- "Lord God, Your Love Has Called Us Here," by Brian Wren
- "When Jesus Wept," by William Billings
- "The Fragrance of Christ," by David Haas
- "May You Run and Not Be Weary," by Paul Murakami and Handt Hanson
- "Change My Heart, O God," by Eddie Espinosa
- "I Have Decided to Follow Jesus," Indian Folk Tune
- "Have Thine Own Way, Lord," by Adelaide A. Pollard

Opening the Service

Call to Worship (based on Psalm 130)

Out of the depths we cry to you, O God.
Hear our cry as we come to you this day.

Out of the depths we cry to you, O God.
We come to hear your word spoken anew.
Out of the depths we cry to you, O God.
We wait in hope and proclaim your steadfast love.
Out of the depths we cry to you, O God.
Our souls wait for you, O God,
> **more than those who watch for the morning,**
> **more than those who watch for the morning.**

—*Or*—

Call to Worship (based on Psalm 51:1-12)

Have mercy on us, O God,
Wash us and cleanse us.
Create in us clean hearts, O God,
And put new and right spirits within us.
Restore to us the joy of your salvation,
Grant us willing spirits.

—*Or*—

Call to Worship (based on Isaiah 43:16-21)

Come and hear the good news,
> our God is doing new things,

Do you not perceive it?
Come and hear the good news,
> our God is doing great things,

Do you not perceive it?
Come and hear the good news,
> our God is making a way in the wilderness

Come and join us as we walk the way of God.

—*Or*—

Call to Worship (based on Psalm 126)

The Lord has done great things for us,
We are like people who dream,
> **seeing visions of a new world.**

Our mouths are filled with laughter.
We shout with joy as we proclaim God's mighty acts.
The Lord has done great things for us,
and we rejoice.

Confession and Pardon

Invite people into a time of reflection with the singing of "Ubi Caritas (Live in Charity)" from the Taizé community. Sing it through a number of times, until there is a sense of that gathered community. The worship leader will then offer bidding prayers, asking people to reflect on the ways that they have fallen short of God's call and hope for them. This will be followed by a period of silence that will end with a verse of "Live in Charity." Another prayer will then be offered and the pattern repeated.

Litany of Confession

All: "Live in Charity" (*Repeat several times*)
Leader: We come as your people, gracious God.
Be with us as we bend the knees of our hearts
to confess the ways that we have
broken your heart.
We have
followed our way, not yours.
We have
ignored your calls to walk
in the way that leads to light and life.

Silence

All: "Live in Charity" (*One verse*)
Leader: We have chosen
words of anger and the way of war
instead of the path of peace.

Silence

All: "Live in Charity" (*One verse*)
Leader: We have
turned away from the children you love,
ignoring and rejecting the poor and needy,
loving things more than people.

91

Silence

    All: **"Live in Charity"** *(One verse)*
    Leader: We offer these our prayers knowing that you
              are always ready to forgive.
              You, who have written
              your law of love in our hearts,
              have declared that you will
              remember our sin no more.
              Create in us clean hearts, and fill us
              with new spirits of love and charity.
    All: **"Live in Charity"** *(Repeat three times)*

Words of Assurance and Pardon

Filled with God's Spirit we are able to live in charity.
May the grace of God fill us with love
    and strengthen us on this our Lenten journey.
With clean hearts and new spirits
    we will rejoice in God's forgiveness.
Amen.

Closing the Service

May the God who made a path in the mighty waters
    be with us as we walk the path of love.
God has done great things for us.
May the son, Jesus, who is the resurrection and the life
    be with us as we prepare to walk the way of the cross.
God has done great things for us.
And may God, the Holy Spirit,
    Restore us, sustain us, and fill us with joy,
        now and always.
Thanks be to God who has done great things for us.

SCRIPTURE INDEX